THE
BABY BISTRO
COOKBOOK

HEALTHY, DELICIOUS CUISINE
FOR BABIES, TODDLERS, AND YOU

BY JOOHEE MUROMCEW

RODALE

© 2003 by Joohee Muromcew
Illustrations © 2003 by Judy Newhouse

Printed in the United States of America
Rodale Inc. makes every effort to use acid-free ∞, recycled paper ♻.

Book design by Carol Angstadt

Library of Congress Cataloging-in-Publication Data

Muromcew, Joohee.
    The baby bistro cookbook : healthy, delicious cuisine for babies, toddlers, and you / Joohee Muromcew.
        p.   cm.
    Includes index.
    ISBN 1–57954–722–2 hardcover
    1. Cookery (Baby foods)   I. Title.
TX740.M837   2003
641.5'622—dc21   2002155819

Distributed to the book trade by St. Martin's Press

    6 8 10 9 7 5   hardcover

RODALE

WE **INSPIRE** AND **ENABLE** PEOPLE TO IMPROVE
THEIR LIVES AND THE WORLD AROUND THEM

FOR MORE OF OUR PRODUCTS
WWW.**RODALESTORE**.COM
(800) 848-4735

To my husband, Alex,

whose love gives me

the courage to succeed.

And for our son, Alexei,

whose boundless joy

and laughter inspire us

to be great parents.

CONTENTS

ACKNOWLEDGMENTS

I'd like to express deepest thanks to:

Mike Cannon and Tony Freund, my friends and mentors at *Town & Country* magazine who provided that much-needed early guidance and encouragement when this book was just an idea.

Nancy Crossman, my agent and a real-life Supermom, who recognized the genuine need for this book and helped me realize its full potential.

Dr. Stephen Rosenbaum, our trusted pediatrician, who always dispenses his no-nonsense parenting advice with affection, humor, and wit.

Old friends from New York and new friends in San Francisco for their countless ideas, introductions, and enthusiasm: Cynthia Richards, Michiko Conklin, Victoria Prendergast, Stella Kapur, Sun Kim, Chanda Chapin, Mary Taylor, Tom Farley, Kristen Carr, and Eric Paul Fournier.

And many hugs and thanks to my team of tiny taste testers who endured all those strange tastes and textures: Gus Richards, Daniel Prendergast, and Jack Conklin.

CHAPTER 1

THE BIRTH OF *THE BABY BISTRO COOKBOOK*

During a routine checkup for our then 9-month-old baby, Alexei, I asked our pediatrician why Alexei didn't like eating his solid food. He'd sailed through the applesauce and yogurt stage, but had since refused meats and vegetables. "It probably doesn't taste very good," was Dr. Rosenbaum's matter-of-fact reply.

He was right. I was diligently making all of Alexei's food myself, but pureed tofu and green beans tastes as unappetizing as it sounds even if it is homemade and organic. That's when I started to cook for Alexei as I have always done for myself and my husband—meals that are healthy, made with organic ingredients, and delicious yet simply prepared. With Alexei's first smiling mouthful of baby ratatouille, I knew our little gourmand had a taste for great cuisine. Pretty soon other moms were peering into Alexei's lunch pack and asking with great curiosity about this "cooking for your baby" thing. Many mothers said that they would cook for their babies and toddlers if they knew how. Of course, these women knew how but just needed some ideas to get started. That's when I started writing *The Baby Bistro Cookbook*.

Is it more work to cook for your child than to feed him out of a jar? Absolutely. It does take a little time and effort, just like anything you do for him. But nothing is more rewarding than knowing that you've given him the best there is. Will you spend the rest of your life in the kitchen? Absolutely not. Do what you can and think realistically about how much you can accomplish before going haywire. Keep in mind that the simplest dishes, even pureed fruits, are fresher and retain more of their vitamins and minerals than commercially made baby food in jars. Teach your children from an early age that healthy, naturally tasty foods can be just as yummy as the nutritionally empty, overprocessed foods that are so temptingly packaged at the grocery store.

Thinking outside the jar

Beyond basic strained apples and peaches, I have to admit I was always put off by commercially produced baby food in jars. I can't remember the last time I ate anything out of a jar other than pickles, capers, and mustard. There are some organically made baby foods, and these are a vast improvement, but have you ever tasted some of these "meals"? Pureed turkey with carrots and rice should not be the same color and texture as pureed apricots. It all has the same bland taste of hospital food.

There are some myths we have been led to believe by the jar people.

• Your baby's first solid food will be from a jar. After the initial rice cereal that your baby tries, you probably want to try bananas or applesauce. Instead of buying bananas in a jar, just reach for a fresh banana (that you already have in the house) and mash it up with a fork. If you absolutely want a smooth-as-silk texture, pulse it in the blender for 15 seconds or push it through a sieve. Making a quart of the freshest, purest applesauce by yourself takes only about an hour, including cooling time.

- Jars are the most convenient way to feed your baby. This is true if you shop at a wholesaler and have a dedicated pantry for jars. Otherwise you will be hauling bags of glass jars every 4 days from the grocery store. Then these jars will take up valuable real estate in your cramped pantry. Adding a few more carrots or bananas to your weekly shopping list, cooking for your child as you do for the rest of your family—these are conveniences that will last far longer.

- Your baby will only eat meat and vegetables if they're mixed with fruit. If you read the ingredients of many meat-based meals in jars, you'll quite often find apricots or apples as an ingredient. Also, many books suggest dipping meats and vegetables in fruit to coax your child to eat them. Food doesn't have to be sweet to taste good; it can sometimes be savory, spicy, tangy, or even just have an appealing appearance and texture.

- Feeding your child from jars ensures accurate portions. This is true in that you will always get 4 ounces of food from a 4-ounce jar. But every child will have his own unique appetite, and it changes with every meal. Alexei will devour an entire bowl of split pea soup for lunch, but the next day will only want a slice of cheese. Feed your child what you and your pediatrician think appropriate, not what the manufacturers have packaged for you.

Finding the time

Parenting books and magazines always seem full of helpful suggestions for saving time, but at the end of the day, there's always so much more you wish you had time for. Let's face it: Thoughtfully taking care of your child will consume most, if not all, of your free time. But think carefully about how you spend your time. I'm always amazed to see parents spend endless time and energy shopping for baby clothes, poring over every baby magazine and catalog that arrives in the mail, and filling their children's schedule with play dates. And yet the prospect of cooking a simple, nutritious meal seems frivolous or excessive.

Keep some commonsense ideas in mind.

• Most of these recipes are meant to yield several portions, which can be refrigerated or frozen for later use. A recipe like the chicken and vegetable soup takes just 15 minutes to make and produces 4 cups. Double a recipe and freeze small portions for a stash of convenient meals.

• Many of these recipes are extremely quick and easy. Scrambled eggs with spinach and goat cheese can be made in less than 10 minutes.

• Cook for your child when you are cooking anyway. If you're making spaghetti sauce for the rest of your family, why not find a way for your toddler to enjoy it? Leave out the extra garlic and serve it over fun pasta shapes or pulse it in a blender. I've had a lot of success cooking two versions of a dish like chicken curry at the same time: spicy in a larger pot for the grown-ups, milder in a smaller pot for Alexei.

• Look for time-savers at the grocery store. Buying a bag of prewashed baby spinach will save you the effort of washing and chopping bunches of regular spinach. One of our favorite dinners is rotisserie roasted chicken bought at the market, which makes for very versatile leftovers for the baby.

• Find an hour on a Sunday and cook for the week. Roast some squash in the oven and make a stove-top dish like chili or pasta at the same time. Cool and refrigerate for a week's worth of dinners.

• Keep staples in your pantry. I'll go into more detail in chapter 3, but the value of not having to dress the baby, load her into the car, and drive to the store for something as mundane as pasta is immeasurable.

• Improvise. Don't have goat cheese? Use cream cheese or just skip it altogether. Your child will forgive you. These recipes aren't meant to drive you crazy; they're meant to motivate and offer guidance.

• Experiment. Give your child a taste of your own food as often as you can. You can save the extra-hot salsa for later, but seeing what your child likes can inspire new ideas. Alexei once had a sip of his granddad's split pea soup and loved it. This was definitely not something I would have anticipated, but now I serve it to him fairly often.

On page 6 is a sample calendar of when you might cook and the menus you could quickly put together with refrigerated or frozen portions. Do not try to cook an entire month's worth of food all at once. You'll be in the kitchen for an entire day, come to associate your blender with all evil, and throw this book out the window. Start off slowly with some basics. Once you have frozen portions of basic fruits, vegetables, and some meat dishes, you can just replenish your supply every few days or even once a week.

Cooking Calendar

WEEK ONE	
Sunday Spend 1 hour cooking: • 10 portions peach puree • 10 portions butternut squash	**Monday through Saturday** Serve peaches with yogurt or cereal for breakfast. Serve squash for lunch or at dinner.

WEEK TWO	
Sunday Spend 1 hour cooking: • 2 cups Cheddar cheese sauce • 10 portions chicken chili	**Monday through Saturday** Continue serving peaches at breakfast, lunch, or dinner. Continue serving squash, but now you have some variety. Alternate meals with chicken chili. The cheese sauce comes in handy over quick-cooking baby pasta, rice, even over steamed broccoli florets.

WEEK THREE	
Sunday Spend 1 hour cooking: • 10 portions pureed pears • 10 portions creamed spinach	**Monday through Saturday** At this point you're running low on peaches, so mix some pears into your menus. You still have lots of chicken chili, cheese sauce, and now creamed spinach. There's lots of variety and you're rounding out your child's nutritional needs. Want something different? For dinner try a cheese quesadilla.

WEEK FOUR	
Sunday Spend 1 hour cooking: • 10 portions lamb and leeks • 10 portions glazed carrots	**Monday through Saturday** You're running low on chicken chili, but now you have lots of lamb and leeks for lunches and dinners. Glazed carrots can replace spinach at a few meals. Want something different? Mash a peeled kiwi for a quick breakfast.

You get the idea. Once you start cooking in reasonable quantities for your child, your incremental effort becomes easier.

Can I get that to go?

Feeding your child while traveling is a challenge. Feeding yourself while traveling is a challenge. So use a combination of creativity and resourcefulness. If you're staying at the family summer house for a few weeks, cook some basic meals, a week's worth at a time.

For most of us most of the time, however, we take weekend trips here and there. You don't want to spend your hard-earned vacations pureeing spinach in a hotel kitchenette. Take what you can, especially if you're taking a car trip. Pack a cooler with a few containers of foods. If there is a refrigerator and microwave available to you, then you could pack a fair number of meals and heat them up as you go along.

Otherwise, improvise. For plane trips, I always take a few containers of Alexei's favorite foods. Thirty thousand feet in the air is not the time to test out a new recipe. This is what I usually pack in a small, insulated lunch bag.

Favorite pureed fruits

Chilled yogurt

Toasted cheese sandwich

Milk or juice in a sippy cup

One or two bribes (low-sugar cookies usually)—sometimes you need them!

I try not to buy jarred baby foods once we arrive at our destination. Most hotel rooms have minibars, and you can often request that the hotel empty them to make room for a small amount of perishables. Go to the nearest market or deli and buy a few items, mainly to get through breakfast and snacks.

A loaf of raisin bread

Crackers and breadsticks

A small box of cereal

Milk or juice

Yogurts

Bananas, kiwis

For lunches and dinners, we try to eat at places that serve baby-friendly meals like macaroni and cheese, spaghetti, or omelets. I've become quite bold, even at fancier restaurants, in asking the kitchen to prepare something simple like a bowl of steamed rice or just a bowl of potatoes with some cheese on top. I've also bought these prepared foods at delis and fed Alexei in our hotel rooms.

Fruit salad

Baked yams (mash with fork)

Baked chicken (shred into pieces with your clean hands)

Macaroni and cheese

Lasagna (cut in smaller pieces)

And yes, on occasion, we have bought a jar or two of baby food, and if Alexei is very hungry, he will eat it. However, it is always our last resort.

I think many people let their own nutritional guard down at least a smidgen when they are on vacation. That's part of the pleasure of vacationing. Your trips will be much more enjoyable for everyone if you also let your child have some more leeway than usual on his balanced diet. This is not to say let him survive on popcorn and nachos, but the occasional doughnut for breakfast while on the road or french fries for lunch when you can't find a healthier option is fine. Remember, make judgments and decisions about your child's nutrition based on generalities, spread over weeks or months, rather than specific meals or days.

You can do it.

Remember those first anxiety-ridden days as a new parent? I was pretty sure that I was doing everything wrong, and looking back, there are a few things I would do differently. But I did it, and so did you. There is a pre-conceived notion that anything you do for your child is full of complex decisions and monumental effort. Some things are and some are not. Cooking for your child is not.

I have always liked to cook, but I had no professional training as a chef. I was definitely not striving for Supermom status. But I did have the motivation to do the best for my child. As I say to my friends, "If I can do it, you can do it." You will look back on making simple dishes like butternut squash or bread-crumb cod and wonder why it seemed so intimidating in the first place.

Include your child in *your* life

This sounds like a ridiculous statement, considering that most new parents feel like their babies have consumed their lives altogether. What about the life you had before? You loved to eat, go out to new restaurants, entertain, and cook at home. Why should your child be excluded and left to eat out of a jar? Don't drop your standards just because that's what you assume you have to do.

My husband, Alex, and I made an early commitment to continue our lifestyle, even if we had to make the extra effort to modify it for our baby. Now, baby Alexei travels with us, goes out on occasion, and compared to his usually tired parents, he's more social than either one of us. Most importantly, he enjoys the same delicious foods that we love, and we know for certain that he is truly getting the best there is.

Bon appétit!

CHAPTER 2

ADAPTING RECIPES FOR YOUR CHILD

ach child will respond to tastes and textures differently and at different times. Some 6-month-olds will only want perfectly smooth, textureless foods for months and months while others will want to jump immediately into more adventurous textures. While it's important to constantly try new things, don't push new textures on your child if she is not ready. I've read in many books that it can take up to 10 attempts for a child to warm up to a new dish.

Most recipes in this book can be adapted for children of most ages, with the exception of sandwiches and finger foods inappropriate for infants. Stews, pasta sauces, and vegetables can all be pureed to a smooth consistency, left slightly chunky, or served as prepared for toddlers who will reliably chew their food before swallowing. When your child is an infant, everything will go through your blender or food mill. Then you'll be chopping foods finely before or after cooking. Finally, your child will be eating enough like an adult that you can start worrying about table manners.

Your child's palate will also constantly grow and change. She will probably like sweet fruits and bland cereals first and then progress to salty, savory, and possibly spicy foods next. Try new tastes as often as possible. If your child shows an interest in your food, give her a taste (keep potential allergies in mind, of course). Remember that even the simplest dishes must taste good. So green beans may not be the most exciting dish, but make them as delicious as possible by using the freshest produce and adding just a little butter or spice to make them appetizing. Particularly complex or sophisticated foods ("stinky" cheeses, smoked foods, etc.) can wait.

Allergies and other issues to discuss with your pediatrician

Like most parents, I spend an inordinate amount of time swapping stories and tips about child-raising with other parents. This invaluable support can make all the difference between feeling helpless and feeling confident. Take all these pieces of advice, recipes, and anecdotes with a grain of salt and always refer to your pediatrician for questions regarding your child's health. If your doctor cannot answer questions for you over the phone or if you feel uncomfortable asking what you may feel are stupid questions, then think about interviewing some other practices that can give you this very necessary level of service.

One of the great concerns facing parents is food allergies. While some studies report that a very small percentage of children have food allergies, there is that small group that will react severely, if not fatally, to some foods. It's not an issue to be taken lightly nor on your own. I often hear, "Little Mike (or whoever) started eating peanut butter when he was 9 months old and he's fine, so maybe my child should try some." That may be the case for someone else, but may not be for your child. Ask your doctor when it's safe to introduce particularly allergenic foods. These include:

Peanuts and tree nuts

Shellfish

Strawberries

Eggs

Dairy

Corn

Soy

Wheat

Most of all, don't be shy or embarrassed about letting friends, child care providers, and even well-intentioned family know that your child is not ready to try foods or is allergic. And make certain your child begins to learn this as well. Your 1½-year-old is too young to know what an allergy is, but she will certainly feel a great sense of tragedy if she cannot partake in birthday cake or punch because of an allergy. Be sensitive to this—bring a very special treat for her if you're going to a party where allergenic foods might be served. Always give your child an alternative rather than just saying no.

How much to eat?

How much to feed a child seems to stump a lot of parents. The prospect of feeding too little seems negligent and too much is perhaps too indulgent. Some child-care reference books outline how many ounces of meat, dairy, vegetables, etc., to feed your child in a given day. I find those suggestions to be really unhelpful as I don't weigh Alexei's meals on a food scale. The best person to tell you how much you should feed your child is your child. Keep in mind that we are talking about nutritious foods and not treats or snacks. Those foods should be kept to a minimum.

Consider the amounts of food you eat. You might be satisfied with a salad for lunch one day, but the next crave an enormous steak sandwich. Our appetites are decided not just by our age, but by how active we are and also by how appetizing we find a particular dish. A good rule of thumb is to offer small portions and then offer seconds. I usually put no more than ½ cup of any one food on Alexei's plate. For dinner, for example, he starts with ½ cup of risotto or ½ cup of mashed potatoes and ½ cup of meat loaf. Your child may find a large amount of food unappetizing or get bored while eating it. And when he is done, let him be done. I always ask at least twice if Alexei would like some more of this or more of that, but I don't beg or scold. If he hasn't had enough to eat and is hungry later, I do offer some of the same food, i.e., no holding out for treats.

Here is what we strive for on a daily basis, though we certainly leave a lot of room for interpretation.

Breakfast

1 cup diluted fresh orange juice

1 small banana

1 cup low-sugar cereal with ½ cup whole milk

and/or 2 slices raisin bread toast

and/or 2 slices French toast

Morning snack

Low-sodium or homemade crackers

½ cup raisins

½ cup water or whole milk

Lunch

1 peanut butter and jam sandwich on whole wheat bread

or 1 toasted cheese sandwich (also on whole wheat bread)

1 small piece fresh fruit or ½ cup applesauce

1 cup diluted fresh orange juice or water

Midafternoon snack

Low-sodium or homemade crackers

½ cup water or whole milk

½ banana or apple

Dinner

½–1 cup of a main course like pasta, rice, meat, fish, etc.

1 slice bread or homemade crackers

1 cup whole milk

½ cup applesauce or 1 small banana

Freezing and storage

Doubling recipes is a great way to fill up your freezer or fridge with many weeks' worth of meals. Simply do a little math and use larger pots. Baked goods can be doubled in quantity, but you should still bake in the suggested-size pans, even if you need to bake in batches.

Store enough food in your refrigerator in larger containers to feed to your child over a week's time. Simply spoon out portions as you need them. Freeze the rest as soon as the food is thoroughly cooled.

There are many ways to freeze food. It all depends on how you like to defrost and what you are freezing. Purees are best frozen in ice cube trays with a layer of plastic wrap on top to prevent frost from forming. When these cubes are set, remove them from the trays and store in large plastic bags or freezer-safe storage containers. Each cube is about 2 ounces of food, so this is a very convenient way to defrost very precise portions.

Soups, stews, and other dishes can also be frozen in ice cube trays. Or you can freeze them in freezer- and microwave-safe containers. I buy the small, disposable kind of containers that are inexpensive but can survive freezing, thawing, and the dishwasher for many months. I find this to be very convenient, especially using the 4-ounce or 8-ounce sizes.

You are what you eat, so eat organic!

I can't stress enough the importance of organically grown foods in our diets, especially for our children. We are, as the saying goes, what we eat, and conventionally grown produce and meats can contain antibiotics, hormones, and pesticides. In the San Francisco Bay Area, we are very lucky to have an abundance of organic farmers. Our farmers' market in Ferry Plaza boasts dozens of certified organic farmers with truly pure and healthful foods.

One of my ongoing goals is to eliminate all nonorganic foods from our diet, especially meat. Sanitation issues aside (and there are many of those), an average conventionally raised steer ingests a great deal of processed feed and chemicals before it is slaughtered. It is usually fed a corn-based feed that it is biologically not accustomed to digesting. So to counter this "indigestion" that makes it ill, the steer is given antibiotics. And then it is given hormones to make it grow faster and bigger. Then there are the pesticides in the feed and its environs. It doesn't matter if you eat a filet mignon at a steak house or a hot dog on a street corner—the basic source of most of the country's beef is largely the same.

I buy our beef from the cheerful cowboys at Prather Ranch. They have a completely organic ranch in Northern California where the steer are grass fed and carefully raised so as to never need antibiotics or hormones. Everything they eat and everything grown on the ranch is organic. Not only do I feel better eating such pure, wholesome beef, but it tastes so much better. It's the difference between a sweet-as-summer farmer's stand tomato and those tomatoes at the supermarket that taste like cardboard. Most of all, I feel very confident feeding their beef (and sometimes they have organic lamb and pork) to Alexei. He truly eats the best burger in the world!

Look for organic foods at your grocery store, and if the selection is slim, ask the store management to start stocking them. As we as a country eat healthier, the demand for organic and all-natural food will drive the food industry to provide these choices for us not only in health food stores, but also at conventional grocers. In addition to produce and meats, everything from soup to nuts is now available from organic food companies.

I also try to avoid hydrogenated fats in our diet. This is challenging since they are present in so many products, especially cookies, crackers, and chips. The good news is that many organic food producers are also avoiding these heart-damaging fats in their foods. Be sure to read labels—once you've read the list of ingredients on a box of organic chocolate chip cookies and compared it to a conventionally made brand, you'll never want to eat conventionally made processed food again.

Some of our favorite organic foods come from these companies.

Amy's Kitchen: Frozen dinner entrées including enchiladas, macaroni and cheese, and lasagna

Bearitos: Wonderful tortilla chips. We especially like their blue corn chips

Cascadian Farms: Widely available preserves and jams as well as frozen vegetables

Garden of Eatin': Delicious snacks, chips, and crackers

Hain: Crackers, soups, and beans

Health Valley: Cereals, granola bars, and canned soups

Muir Glen: Widely available canned tomatoes, tomato sauce, and salsa

Newman's Own: Aside from the salsa and spaghetti sauce, Paul Newman's ever-charitable company has a line of organic pretzels, cookies, and snacks

Shari's: Canned vegetables, beans, and soups. Great canned pumpkin in the fall

CHAPTER 3

PREPARATION IS KEY

As with anything, being organized takes half of the effort out of cooking for your little one. Below are simple suggestions for turning your kitchen into an efficient food preparation center.

The staples

Nothing deflates the motivation to cook more quickly than a trip to the supermarket. The recipes in this book do not require any exotic ingredients or obscure spices, and for the most part, call for items that most families will have in their cupboards and refrigerators. To prevent last-minute trips to the market, be prepared by having some staples on hand in your pantry, refrigerator, and freezer.

Pantry (unperishable items)

> Pasta (spaghetti and fun shapes)
>
> Brown and white rice
>
> All-purpose flour

Whole wheat flour

Baking powder

Baking soda

Cornmeal

Bread crumbs (or crackers to crush)

Spices, especially cinnamon and sweet paprika

Salt and pepper

Olive oil

Vegetable oil

Refrigerator (perishables, to buy every other trip to the market)

Whole milk

Plain yogurt

Butter

Shredded Cheddar cheese

Onions

Potatoes

Baby carrots

Bananas

Apples

Freezer

Peas

Mixed vegetables

Ground beef, chicken, and turkey

TERROR IN AISLE THREE:
Taking Your Child to the Supermarket

I've vowed many times to never, ever again take Alexei to the supermarket. Of course, there have been many times we've gone there, quickly done our shopping, and gotten away without major incident. But far too often for my sanity, our trips to the market have turned into miserable battles between Alexei wanting to get out of the cart or touch everything he can and me trying to get through a crowded checkout line, pretending I don't know this screaming terror.

The best option is to leave your child at home with a sitter or spouse. Consider doing your grocery shopping at night, when your spouse might be tucking your tot into bed with a story. The stores are also very quiet at night.

But for many of us, evenings are the last remnants of our day, and I always look forward to a couple of hours with my husband after Alexei's gone to bed. So if your schedule requires you to take your child to the supermarket, keep a few things in mind.

- Don't take him when he's tired or hungry. There's no cure for cranky.

- A supermarket is a very interesting place for babies and toddlers, full of sights, sounds, and smells to explore. Let him touch the items you are putting into the cart.

- Be prepared to give him a treat or snack. Those bright boxes of cookies and aisles of potato chips would pique anyone's appetite. Either bring along a small snack or make a healthy store-bought treat something to look for. ("Is this is where the animal crackers live? No, it's the laundry detergent! Let's keep looking.")

- Make a list before you go. This will cut down on the time spent in the store and the number of times you crisscross the floor to retrieve an item you suddenly realize you need.

- Despite whatever you do in the store, sitting in a steel cart can be boring and confining. Have an activity, however brief, to look forward to after the store. Your perishable items, if they are bagged with frozen items, can keep in the car for a half hour or so while your toddler lets off some steam in a nearby park.

Kitchen equipment

One of my pet peeves is cleaning kitchen equipment. I'm not a big fan of fancy gadgets that have complex assembly or cleaning requirements, and you can quickly lose your enthusiasm for a recipe if it requires you to have a certain piece of equipment. So most of these recipes require nothing more sophisticated than a blender. You can use a food mill, and these are inexpensively bought for very smooth purees, but I've never really found a need for one. You can also use a food processor for pureeing or chopping, but I find it easier to rinse a blender than to disassemble an enormous food processor and clean every blade and attachment. There are some very basic things you should have in the kitchen to make cooking easier and more efficient. You probably have most of these items already.

• **Sharp knives.** I can't say enough about how much easier and safer it is to use sharp knives. They needn't be expensive, as long as the handle is sturdy and you keep the blade honed. A dull blade will make slicing and chopping a much harder task, so sharpen your knives frequently.

• **Measuring cups and spoons.** For baking these are a must because of the precise chemistry involved in raising a cake, for example, or browning cookies.

• **Nonstick skillet.** You'll use less oil and cleanup is easier. In fact, many nonstick pan manufacturers recommend just wiping the pan with a damp sponge.

• **Parchment paper.** I use this quite a lot to line baking sheets. Food won't stick, and you can just throw the parchment paper away after use.

• **Baking sheets and pans.** You'll use these for baking and roasting. I find a good basic set consists of one baking sheet, at least one or two cake pans, and then a large baking pan for cakes or roasting. Look for nonstick.

- **Whisk.** Good for making whipped cream but also a good tool for creating lots of volume in icings and frostings.

- **Rubber spatula.** I have two or three on hand. They can cleanly scrape out every last bit of food from bowls, blenders, and pots.

- **Wooden spoons.** Your child has probably already put these to good use playing percussion on the kitchen floor. They are indispensable for mixing and cooking over heat.

- **Ice cube trays.** These are indispensable for freezing and consistently hold about 2 ounces of food per cube.

- **Plastic storage containers.** I buy the cheaper, disposable kind at our warehouse club. The smaller ones are perfect for freezing small portions and the larger ones are good for refrigerating a week's worth of food.

- **Plastic food storage bags.** For packing snacks and for freezing foods like veggie burgers and cooked vegetables.

- **Oil spray can.** It did look like a gimmicky gadget at first, but I use ours quite a lot for a minimal spray of oil on frying pans or to very lightly coat food with oil.

A place for jarred baby food

The whole motivation for this cookbook was to get parents away from commercially made jarred baby food. But I must confess that if you were to have looked through our recycling, you would have found a telltale jar or two. As I often tell (scream at) my husband, "I'm not Superwoman!" Sometimes I just don't have the motivation to cook, so we get takeout, and indeed Alexei did occasionally have jars of food when I was too tired to prepare something fresh or too unorganized to realize we were out of

HEALTHY FINGER FOODS

Keep these easy foods on hand for quick snacking.

Baby carrots

Low-sugar graham crackers (without hydrogenated fat)

Low-sodium crackers (without hydrogenated fat)

A healthy cereal for snacking (Quaker Oatmeal Squares, Cheerios, Puffins, Weetabix, etc.)

Sunflower seeds (for older toddlers)

Baked peas or mild Japanese-style roasted peas (for older toddlers)

Dried fruit—raisins, apricots, apples, apricots

Banana chips (for older toddlers)

Fig bars (without hydrogenated fat)

Low-sodium pretzels (for older toddlers)

Popcorn (for older toddlers)

homemade baby food. Our culture demands a great deal from parents, especially moms. Whether you work or not, it is difficult to maintain a high quality of child-raising while still carrying on with your household and life's demands. We simply can't do it all, all the time. Consider those jars to be your backup, like the jar of spaghetti sauce you keep for busy nights. And always try to buy organic (Earth's Best and Gerber both produce organic baby food).

The other very important place for jarred food is in any emergency kit. Many Californians have emergency earthquake kits in preparation for the "big one." Every family, no matter where you live, can benefit from having a few necessities tucked away in case of an emergency. Your family's needs for such a kit will depend on where you live and what kind of disaster you're planning for. Check with the Red Cross or your local fire department about what to include for your needs. A few things we packed specifically for our toddler are:

Canned fruit, vegetables, and beans (jars of baby food if your child is still eating it)

A box of granola bars

Powdered milk and juice boxes

Lots of water

A change of clothes

Diapers

A set of basic medication

Remember to update your kit as your child grows and to replenish your food supply. Even canned food can expire.

CHAPTER 4

FRUITS AND VEGETABLES

Your child's first taste of fruit will probably be applesauce, and I hope you will try making it from fresh, organic apples rather than buying it in jars. If you seek out perfect produce for yourself at the market, then your child should eat foods just as delicious and nutritionally robust. As your child grows, consider7 fruits and many vegetables as nature's convenience food—no need to wash, cook, or even in some cases, peel. Snacks needn't be any more processed than a peeled banana or a washed pear.

Every parent I spoke to about infant and toddler nutrition wished their child ate more vegetables. Indeed, I think we as adults probably need to eat more vegetables. The key is to make vegetables taste good from the beginning and to pace your introduction of newer textures and tastes. Your 2-year-old doesn't like boiled Brussels sprouts? Gee, I wonder why. Most adults don't like them either. Try crunchy, naturally sweet sugar snap peas or some mild cauliflower with a sprinkle of Cheddar cheese. Whatever you serve your child, taste it and ask yourself if you would eat it, too.

In this chapter...

APPLESAUCE

For many babies, applesauce is their first taste of fruit. It's so simple to make, even in large quantities, why not give your child the freshest purees? Applesauce is still one of Alexei's favorite snacks. Any apple variety will work except Granny Smith, which will have your child puckering with its sour taste. Double or triple this recipe as your time and freezer space allow.

> 8 apples of any variety (our favorites are Fuji apples)

For infants, peel and core the apples. The peel can be left on for toddlers. Cut the apples into quarters.

Put the apples in a large pot with 1" water. Cover and bring to a boil over medium-high heat. Reduce the heat to low and simmer for 10–15 minutes or until the apples are tender but not mushy. The temptation is always to let the apples cook until they are of applesauce consistency, but you will end up with a watery mess that is drained of flavor.

Uncover and let the apples cool slightly in the pot. In batches, puree the apples and a few tablespoons of the cooking water in a blender or food processor to a consistency appropriate for your child. Pour the applesauce into storage containers or ice cube trays (see note on the opposite page about freezing). Let cool completely before refrigerating or freezing. Store in the refrigerator for up to 1 week or freeze for up to 3 months.

Makes about 2½ cups

BISTRO BITS: To freeze pureed fruit, pour it into ice cube trays. Cover with a layer of plastic wrap. Freeze until set.

Store your cubes of fruit in freezer-safe storage containers or plastic bags. I found that keeping it in the trays was messy and the fruit was quickly covered in frost.

FUN FRUIT SNACKS

Apple Fans with Cheese

Each fan is a quarter of an apple. Slice an apple into quarters, then remove the core from each quarter. Make three lengthwise cuts into each quarter, leaving a ½" "hinge" on one end. Spread gently to fan out the slices. Insert thin slices of Cheddar cheese between the apple slices.

Melon Balls

Cut a cantaloupe or honeydew melon in half and remove the seeds and pulp. Using a melon baller, gently scoop out balls, starting from the center. Serve in a cup with a fork.

Kiwi Cups

Slice a kiwi in half and serve each half with a small spoon. For smaller children, gently mash the kiwi flesh first with a fork, being careful not to tear the skin.

PUREED SUMMER FRUITS

We are very fortunate in San Francisco to have the Saturday morning Ferry Plaza Farmers' Market. It represents so much of the good life in Northern California. During the summer months we load up on as much ripe fruit as we can carry.

3   pounds fresh plums, peaches, apricots, or
    nectarines

If your fruit is organically grown, then leave the skin on after a thorough rinse. If your fruit is not organically grown, peel the fruit.

Cut the fruit into chunks, discarding the pits.

Put the fruit in a steamer basket in a large pot with 1" water. Cover and bring to a boil over medium-high heat. Reduce the heat to medium and steam for 10 minutes or until the fruit is soft but not mushy. Uncover and let the fruit cool slightly in the pot. In batches, puree the fruit in a blender or food processor to a consistency appropriate for your child. Pour the fruit puree into storage containers or ice cube trays (see note about freezing on page 29). Let cool completely before refrigerating or freezing. Store in the refrigerator for up to 1 week or freeze for up to 3 months.

Makes about 6 cups

BISTRO BITS: You will always have a use for pureed fruit, so double or triple this recipe and freeze it for weeks of quick breakfasts and desserts. This is especially useful if your baby's favorite fruit is seasonal. Alexei had an early taste for white peaches.

DELICATE FRESH FRUITS

Some fruits are best enjoyed without cooking. These mostly tropical fruits will break down into a flavorless mess if you steam them. A food mill is handy if your child is in the pureed foods stage. Otherwise, dicing them into small cubes is as much preparation as these perfect foods call for.

- Banana
- Honeydew melon and cantaloupe
- Kiwi
- Mango
- Papaya
- Pineapple
- Star fruit
- Strawberries and blueberries

Look for more fruit recipes in the Breakfast and Brunch chapter (page 60) and the Snacks and Beverages chapter (page 140).

Pureed Pears

A very ripe pear can be easily mashed with a fork, after the skin and seeds are removed, without steaming. This recipe, however, will give you up to 3 cups of mildly sweet puree.

8 ripe pears

For infants, peel and core the pears. The peel can be left on for toddlers. Cut the pears into quarters.

Put the pears in a large pot with 1" water. Cover and bring to a boil over medium-high heat. Reduce the heat to low and simmer for 5–10 minutes or until the pears are tender but not mushy. Ripe pears are naturally soft, so it is quite easy to overcook them.

Uncover and let the pears cool slightly in the pot. In batches, puree the pears and a few tablespoons of the cooking water in a blender or food processor to a consistency appropriate for your child. Pour the pear puree into storage containers or ice cube trays (see note on page 29 about freezing). Let cool completely before refrigerating or freezing. Store in the refrigerator for up to 1 week or freeze for up to 3 months.

Makes about 2½ cups

BISTRO BITS: Pureed fruit is itself a wonderful ingredient. It's the easiest, freshest way to flavor oatmeal, rice cereal, yogurt, or soy or cow's milk.

Pureed Peas

The taste of freshly shelled peas is incomparably sweet and summery. But these seasonal treats make very brief appearances at the farmers' market. Use high-quality frozen peas if you like and look for organic.

2 cups frozen thawed or fresh peas
1 wedge lemon

Put a steamer basket in a large saucepan with 1" water. Bring to a boil over medium-high heat. Reduce the heat to medium. Add the peas, then squeeze the lemon wedge over the peas (this will enliven their flavor and help retain their color). Cover and steam for 3–5 minutes or until the peas are tender. The peas should be bright green. Uncover and let the peas cool slightly in the pot. In batches, puree the peas in a blender or food processor, adding some of the steaming water if needed to loosen the texture of the puree. Pour the pea puree into storage containers or ice cube trays (see note on page 29 about freezing). Let cool completely before refrigerating or freezing. Store in the refrigerator for up to 1 week or freeze for up to 3 months.

Makes about 1½ cups

PUREED SUGAR SNAP PEAS

While regular green beans are better steamed, sugar snap peas make a delicious puree if you remove the string from the pod.

½ pound fresh sugar snap peas
1 wedge lemon

Trim the woody ends of the sugar snap peas, pulling and discarding the string from the side of the pod. Put a steamer basket in a large saucepan with 1" water. Bring to a boil over medium-high heat. Reduce the heat to medium. Add the peas, then squeeze the lemon wedge over the peas (this will enliven their flavor and help retain their color). Cover and steam for 3–5 minutes or until the peas are tender. The peas will be bright green and "sweating." Uncover and let the peas cool slightly in the pot. In batches, puree the peas in a blender or food processor, adding some of the steaming water if needed to loosen the texture of the puree. Pour the pea puree into storage containers or ice cube trays (see note on page 29 about freezing). Let cool completely before refrigerating or freezing. Store in the refrigerator for up to 1 week or freeze for up to 3 months.

Makes about 1½ cups

STEAMED GREEN BEANS

Green beans, to be quite honest, just don't taste so great when pureed. Their stringy texture and wholly "vegetable" taste don't translate well into a puree. I think they're best served fresh, not frozen, and lightly steamed with butter and a little salt. A good pick-up food for little fingers.

½ pound green beans, preferably fresh
1 wedge lemon
1 tablespoon butter
   Salt to taste

Trim the woody ends of the green beans with a sharp knife or shears. Put a steamer basket in a large saucepan with 1" water. Bring to a boil over medium-high heat. Reduce the heat to medium. Add the green beans, then squeeze the lemon wedge over the beans (this will enliven their flavor and help retain their color). Cover and steam for 10 minutes or until the beans are tender. Remove the beans to a serving bowl. Add the butter and sprinkle with salt. Toss to coat.

Makes about 2 cups

ZUCCHINI AND YELLOW SQUASH PUREE

Don't ever peel zucchini or yellow squash. Most of the flavor and nutrients are in the skin. A brisk scrub under running water should remove any dirt.

1   pound zucchini and/or yellow squash, cut into 1" rounds
1   wedge lemon

Put a steamer basket in a large saucepan with 1" water. Bring to a boil over medium-high heat. Reduce the heat to medium. Add the zucchini and squash and squeeze the lemon wedge over the zucchini and squash (this will enliven their flavor). Cover and steam for 5 minutes or until the zucchini and squash is tender. Uncover and let the zucchini and squash cool slightly in the pot. In batches, puree in a blender or food processor. Squash tends to release quite a lot of its own water, so you shouldn't need to add any water to loosen the texture. Pour the zucchini and squash puree into storage containers or ice cube trays (see note on page 29 about freezing). Let cool completely before refrigerating or freezing. Store in the refrigerator for up to 1 week or freeze for up to 3 months.

Makes about 2 cups

Edamame

Soybeans are a healthy and surprisingly fun food. Little hands love to open up the pods and pick out each little bean.

    1 pound fresh or frozen thawed edamame or green soybeans
  ½ teaspoon salt

Put a steamer basket in a large saucepan with 1" water. Bring to a boil over medium-high heat. Reduce the heat to medium. Add the beans and sprinkle with the salt. Cover and steam for 10 minutes or until the beans are warmed through. Uncover and let the beans cool. To serve, remove and discard the tough, stringy pods and eat the beans inside.

Makes about 3 cups

PUREED CARROTS

I use baby carrots for their sweet flavor and to skip the peeling.

1 pound baby carrots
1 wedge lemon

Put a steamer basket in a large saucepan with 1" water. Bring to a boil over medium-high heat. Reduce the heat to medium. Add the carrots, then squeeze the lemon wedge over the carrots (this will enliven their flavor). Cover and steam for 10 minutes or until the carrots are tender. Uncover and let the carrots cool slightly in the pot. In batches, puree the carrots in a blender or food processor, adding some of the steaming water if needed to loosen the texture of the puree. Pour the carrot puree into storage containers or ice cube trays (see note on page 29 about freezing). Let cool completely before refrigerating or freezing. Store in the refrigerator for up to 1 week or freeze for up to 3 months.

Makes about 2 cups

STEAMED BABY-CARROT TEETHING SNACKS

Serve a few of these to your teething toddler to gnaw on (keep an eye on him, of course). It just might be the moment to get him hooked on carrots.

½ pound baby carrots
1 wedge lemon

Put a steamer basket in a large saucepan with 1" water. Bring to a boil over medium-high heat. Reduce the heat to medium. Add the carrots, then squeeze the lemon wedge over the carrots (this will enliven their flavor). Cover and steam for 4 minutes or until the carrots are slightly tender. Rinse the carrots under running cold water until cool. Put any leftover carrots in a storage container and refrigerate for up to 4 days.

Makes about 1 cup

APPLE CIDER–GLAZED CARROTS

I know some parents sprinkle a little brown sugar on steamed carrots to entice their children. Save the sugar for special occasions and try this recipe for a naturally sweet vegetable dish.

> 1 cup baby carrots, quartered lengthwise
> ½ cup apple cider
> 1 tablespoon butter

Put a steamer basket in a medium saucepan with 1" water. Bring to a boil over medium-high heat. Reduce the heat to medium. Add the carrots, cover, and steam for 10 minutes or until tender but not mushy. Drain the carrots and keep warm. In the same saucepan bring the apple cider and butter to a boil over medium-high heat. Return the carrots to the pan and toss until glazed.

Serve as a delectable first finger food or mash to a consistency appropriate for your child.

Makes about 1½ cups

BISTRO BITS: This recipe makes enough for a week's worth of snacks or side dishes. If you want to freeze it, cool the carrots completely and throw them into a plastic bag. Easy!

OVEN-ROASTED ROOT VEGETABLES

The natural sugars in parsnips, turnips, and carrots achieve glorious warmth when roasted.

2 pounds root vegetables, such as parsnips, turnips, or carrots, peeled and chopped into 1" pieces

1 tablespoon olive oil

Preheat the oven to 350°F.

In a large bowl, toss the vegetables with the olive oil until evenly coated. Spread in 1 layer on a baking sheet.

Roast in the oven for 30 minutes or until the vegetables are tender when pierced with a fork.

Serve as a finger food or mash to a consistency appropriate for your child.

Makes about 5 cups

BISTRO BITS

- These vegetables are a cinch to freeze. Let the vegetables cool completely and then throw into a plastic bag. Or, freeze the puree in ice cube trays.

- These are a staple in Alexei's diet. As a variation, fill a small ramekin with puree, top with Cheddar cheese, and bake in a 350°F oven for 15 minutes. Or puree and simmer with low-sodium chicken broth for an easy, nutritious soup.

Roasted Beets

Don't the roasted baby beets always sound so good at fancy restaurants? Why not make these simple, naturally sweet treats at home? They are as simple to make as baked potatoes.

8–10 small or baby beets, unpeeled and
scrubbed

Preheat the oven to 350°F.

Trim the beet tops to within 1" of the beets. Wrap the beets in aluminum foil and place on a baking sheet. Bake for 1 hour or until very tender. Remove them from the oven and let cool until you can safely handle them. Remove the beets from the foil and remove and discard the skins. Serve the beets whole, cut into wedges, or diced.

Makes about 2 cups

BISTRO BITS: You can either discard the beet tops or save them to serve to the rest of your family. They have a pleasantly bitter taste, like a broccoli rabe or Swiss chard. Roughly chop and sauté with a little olive oil and garlic.

Parsnip Sticks

This yummy root vegetable can stand in for potatoes. I like them baked like oven fries.

> 3 large parsnips, peeled and trimmed
> 2 tablespoons olive oil
> Salt to taste

Preheat the oven to 400°F. Line a baking sheet with parchment paper.

Cut the parsnips lengthwise in half, then into lengthwise quarters. Remove and discard the fibrous core. Cut the parsnips into ½" sticks. In a large bowl, toss the parsnip sticks with the oil and salt. Put them onto the baking sheet, spreading in a single layer. Bake for 10 minutes. Turn the sticks over and bake for another 10 minutes or until crispy on the outside and soft inside. Remove the pan to a wire rack and let cool slightly.

Makes about 2 cups

Baked Sweet Potato Sticks

These delicious snacks are a healthier alternative to french fries and flavorful enough for the whole family.

2 large sweet potatoes, unpeeled and scrubbed
1 tablespoon vegetable oil

Preheat the oven to 400°F. Line a baking sheet with parchment paper.

Cut the potatoes into ½"-thick sticks. In a large bowl, toss the potatoes with the vegetable oil until coated. Put them onto the baking sheet, spreading in a single layer. Bake for 10 minutes. Turn the sticks over and bake for another 10 minutes or until crispy on the outside and soft inside. Remove pan to a wire rack and let cool slightly.

Makes about 3 cups

Mashed Yams

You can cook these potatoes like traditional ones in a pot of water, but then some of the nutrients leach out into the cooking water. Steaming them as shown below retains all of the nutrients.

3 small yams or sweet potatoes, peeled

Cut the yams or sweet potatoes into large chunks. Put a steamer basket in a large saucepan with 1" water. Bring to a boil over medium-high heat. Reduce the heat to medium. Add the sweet potatoes, cover, and steam for 15 minutes or until tender. Uncover and let the yams or sweet potatoes cool slightly in the pot. In batches, puree the potatoes in a blender or food processor, adding some of the boiling water if needed to loosen the texture of the puree. Pour the potato puree into storage containers or ice cube trays (see note on page 29 about freezing). Let cool completely before refrigerating or freezing. Store in the refrigerator for up to 1 week or freeze for up to 3 months.

Makes about 3 cups

BISTRO BITS: When serving mashed yams or sweet potatoes to the whole family, mash the potatoes with a potato masher. Place about ½ cup of the mashed potatoes in the blender or food processor and prepare as above for your infant. Toddlers should be able to eat the mashed version.

Mashed Potatoes

Potatoes are simmered with butter, milk, and a little garlic, then mashed into a melt-in-your-mouth creaminess. When preparing mashed potatoes for infants and younger toddlers, peel the potatoes first.

3 large potatoes, unpeeled and scrubbed
2 tablespoons butter
1 clove garlic, sliced in half
¾ cup milk

Cut the potatoes into large chunks. Put the potatoes in a large saucepan with enough water to cover. Add the butter and garlic and bring to a boil over high heat. Reduce the heat to medium-high and continue boiling for 15 minutes or until the potatoes are tender when pierced with a fork. Drain the potatoes, reserving the boiling water for mashing. Return the potatoes and garlic to the pot on the stove. Add the milk to the potatoes and cook over medium heat for 5 minutes or until heated through. Remove from the heat and discard the garlic. Using a potato masher, mash the potatoes in the pot, adding some of the boiling water if needed to loosen the texture. Pour the potato puree into storage containers or ice cube trays (see note on page 29 about freezing). Let cool completely before re-frigerating or freezing. Store in the refrigerator for up to 1 week or freeze for up to 3 months.

Makes about 2 cups

Scalloped Potatoes

This tender potato dish is best for older toddlers. Refrigerate leftovers in the baking pan and spoon out portions as you need them.

3 medium potatoes, unpeeled and scrubbed
2 tablespoons butter
2 tablespoons all-purpose flour
1 cup milk
½ cup shredded Gruyère or Swiss cheese

Preheat the oven to 375°F. Lightly butter a 2-quart deep baking dish.

Cut the potatoes into ½"-thick slices; set aside. In a small saucepan, melt the butter over medium heat. Reduce the heat to low, add the flour, and cook, stirring constantly, for 2 minutes or until the mixture begins to brown. Gradually stir in the milk. Cook, stirring frequently, for 5 minutes or until the mixture thickens. Reserve 2 tablespoons of the cheese for the topping. Add the remaining cheese to the sauce and cook, stirring constantly, until the cheese is melted. Remove from the heat and set aside.

Layer half of the potatoes in the baking dish, then pour half of the cheese sauce over the potatoes. Repeat with the remaining potatoes and cheese sauce. Sprinkle with the reserved 2 tablespoons of cheese. Bake for 30 minutes or until the potatoes are bubbling around the edges and the top is golden brown.

Makes about 5 cups

TWICE-BAKED POTATOES

Each stuffed potato half makes a hearty dinner. Leftover broccoli, corn, peas, or green beans round out this dish.

2 large baking potatoes
½ cup milk
1 tablespoon butter
½ cup finely chopped, cooked vegetables
½ cup shredded Cheddar cheese

Preheat the oven to 400°F.

Pierce the potatoes a few times with a fork or knife. Wrap each potato in aluminum foil and bake directly on the oven rack for about 45 minutes or until very tender. Remove from the oven and let cool until you can safely handle them. Reduce the oven temperature to 350°F. Slice each potato in half and gently scoop out as much of the potato as possible without puncturing the skin.

In a large bowl, mash together the potato flesh, milk, and butter. Stir in the vegetables and ¼ cup of the cheese. Evenly fill each potato skin with the potato mixture, mounding it over the edge, if necessary. Sprinkle each with 1 tablespoon of the remaining cheese. Place the potatoes on a baking sheet and bake for 20 minutes or until heated through and the cheese is melted and slightly browned.

Makes 4 potato halves

CRISPY CAULIFLOWER

I consider cauliflower a vastly underrated vegetable, especially for children. It has a mild, some would say bland, flavor and a pleasingly soft texture. It also wonderfully absorbs spices and sauces.

½ head of cauliflower, broken into small florets
2 tablespoons vegetable oil
½ teaspoon sweet paprika
Salt to taste

Wash and thoroughly dry the cauliflower with paper towels. In a large skillet, heat the oil over medium-high heat and cook the cauliflower for about 6 minutes, turning once, or until lightly browned and crispy. Sprinkle with the paprika and season with salt.

Makes about 2 cups

Asparagus with Hollandaise

It's not exactly hollandaise. True hollandaise is very tricky to prepare while keeping the recipe free from any possible salmonella. Asparagus makes a fun finger food, especially with this eye-popping yellow sauce.

1 bunch asparagus, trimmed
1 lemon, halved
2 tablespoons butter
1 tablespoon all-purpose flour
1 cup milk
1 egg yolk

In a large saucepan, combine the asparagus, the juice of half of the lemon, and about 1" water. Cover and bring to a boil over medium-high heat. Reduce the heat to medium and cook for 2 minutes or until the asparagus is bright green and crisp-tender. Rinse the asparagus under running cold water until cool, then drain.

In a small saucepan, melt the butter over medium heat. Reduce the heat to low, add the flour, and cook, stirring constantly, for 2 minutes or until the mixture is bubbly. Stir in the milk and cook, stirring frequently, for 5 minutes or until the milk thickens. Meanwhile, place the egg yolk in a medium bowl.

While whisking the yolk constantly, slowly pour ½ cup of the warm milk mixture into the egg yolk. Continue whisking until smooth and yellow. While whisking the remaining milk mixture constantly, slowly return the egg yolk mixture to the saucepan. Continue to cook, stirring frequently, for about 5 minutes, making sure to not let it curdle. Remove from the heat and squeeze in the remaining lemon juice. Cool and serve as a dip for the asparagus.

Makes about 1 cup sauce and 2 cups asparagus

Bistro Bits: Should your sauce curdle, simply pour it through a fine strainer to remove any cooked egg.

Steamed Broccoli with Cheddar Cheese

2 cups broccoli florets
½ cup shredded Cheddar cheese

Put a steamer basket in a medium saucepan with 1" water. Bring to a boil over medium-high heat. Reduce the heat to medium and add the broccoli florets. Cover and steam for 2 minutes or until crisp-tender. Uncover and sprinkle the cheese over the broccoli. Cover, remove from the heat, and let stand until the cheese is melted.

Makes 2 cups

CURRIED BUTTERNUT SQUASH

Roasted butternut squash is so naturally sweet and rich, it's a great base to add newer, more exotic flavors. We eat quite a lot of Indian food at home, so I wanted Alexei to like curry from an early age.

1 butternut squash
½–1 teaspoon mild curry powder
1 tablespoon maple syrup

Preheat the oven to 400°F.

Cut the squash in half lengthwise and scoop out the seeds. Place the cut side down in a baking dish filled with ½" water.

Bake for 30–45 minutes or until the squash is tender when pierced with a fork. Remove from the oven and let cool until you can safely handle it.

Using a large spoon, gently scoop the squash from the skin and place it in a large bowl with the curry powder and maple syrup.

Mash and stir until smooth.

Makes about 2½ cups

BISTRO BITS

- Though this recipe makes a week's worth of a great standby side dish, it also freezes well in ice cube trays.
- Most curry powders have some amount of cayenne pepper and other spicy ingredients, so don't sprinkle it on finger foods. It's painfully hot if it gets in eyes.
- When Alexei is having a finicky moment (every day, really), I have been able to successfully feed him fish and plain chicken breast by hiding them in this dish.

CREAMED SPINACH

I love the rich, creamed spinach served at steak houses. This version is made with milk rather than cream, but is just as delicious.

        1   tablespoon olive oil
        1   bag prewashed fresh spinach
        2   tablespoons butter
        2   tablespoons all-purpose flour
    1½   cups milk
            Salt to taste

In a large skillet, heat the oil over medium-high heat. Add the spinach and cook, quickly working the spinach down with tongs or a wooden spoon, until wilted but still bright green. Remove the spinach to a plate and cool.

In the same skillet, melt the butter over medium heat. Reduce the heat to low, add the flour, and cook, stirring constantly, for 2 minutes or until the mixture is bubbly. Stir in the milk and cook, stirring frequently, for 5 minutes or until the mixture thickens. Return the spinach to the skillet, stir, and season with salt. Let the spinach cool slightly in the skillet. For infants, in batches, puree in a blender or food processor.

Makes about 2 cups

PALAK PANEER
(CURRIED SPINACH AND CHEESE)

I'm sure that connoisseurs of authentic Indian food will find this a laughably Americanized version of the spicy original. This is a surprise hit with children who like robust flavors.

　1　tablespoon olive oil
　1　bag prewashed fresh spinach
　2　tablespoons butter
　2　tablespoons all-purpose flour
　1　teaspoon mild curry powder
1½　cups milk
　2　ounces mozzarella cheese, cut into ½" cubes (about ½ cup)
　　　Hot cooked rice

In a large skillet, heat the oil over medium-high heat. Add the spinach and cook, quickly working the spinach down with tongs or a wooden spoon, until wilted but still bright green. Remove the spinach to a plate and cool.

In the same skillet, melt the butter over medium heat. Reduce the heat to low, add the flour and curry powder, and cook, stirring constantly, for 2 minutes or until the mixture is bubbly. Stir in the milk and cook, stirring frequently, for 5 minutes or until the mixture thickens. Return the spinach to the skillet and stir. Let the spinach cool slightly in the skillet. In batches, puree in a blender or food processor. Return the puree to the skillet and stir in the cheese cubes. Serve with rice.

Makes about 2 cups

CORN PUDDING

A delicious, almost dessertlike pudding. You can use frozen or fresh corn for this recipe. Do not use canned—it's too high in sodium.

2 cups milk
3 eggs
1 tablespoon maple syrup
1 cup frozen thawed or fresh corn kernels

Preheat the oven to 350°F.

In a large bowl, whisk together the milk and eggs until smooth and a light lemony color. Gently stir in the syrup and corn. Pour into a 2-quart deep, buttered baking dish. Bake for 40 minutes or until the top is lightly golden and firm to the touch. Cool slightly before serving.

Makes about 3 cups

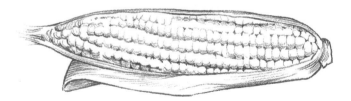

A FRY BABY I AM NOT

Almost all the parents whom I surveyed about their child's eating habits wished their child would eat more vegetables. I asked, "Even if they're fried?" The answer was always yes. It is a challenge to make vegetables appealing to little palates. The subtlety of a mesclun salad is really lost at this age. I have found that vegetable tempura and vegetable fritters are the most reliable compromise between taste and nutrition.

Before these deep-fried encounters, however, I rarely ever fried anything, even eggs. It's just not the way we eat. But here are some things you can do to keep fried foods as nutritionally sound as possible.

- Heat the pan until it's hot. Heat the oil until it's hot. These two steps will decrease the amount of oil that the food absorbs and you will use less oil. A piece of tempura dropped into an inadequately heated pan will soak up oil like a sponge.

- Cook quickly at high temperatures. The appeal of fried food is the crispy coating. Small, fast-cooking foods like zucchini will cook in just 2 to 3 minutes. Carrots, sweet potatoes, and denser vegetables should be cut into small pieces to reduce cooking time. Otherwise, you can do a quick fry and then finish them in a 350°F oven.

Vegetable Tempura

1   cup all-purpose flour
1   egg
1   cup ice water
    Vegetable oil for frying
3   cups your favorite vegetables, such as
    carrots, eggplant, green beans, or peas,
    sliced into pieces no larger than 2"

Preheat the oven to 200°F.

In a large bowl, whisk together the flour, egg, and ice water until blended though still lumpy. In a deep saucepan or fryer, heat at least 3" oil to 375°F. Or test with a few drops of batter. The oil is ready when the batter immediately bubbles and sets. Working in batches, dip a few vegetables in the batter, allowing any excess to drip off, and then place in the oil. Do not crowd the pieces. When the vegetables float to the surface, turn them with tongs and cook until crispy, no longer than 6 minutes. Let drain on paper towels. When frying, be sure to let the oil return to its temperature in between batches.

Put the drained tempura on a baking sheet and keep it warm in the oven. Refrigerate leftovers and reheat them in a toaster oven.

Makes about 3 cups

ZUCCHINI COINS

2 medium zucchini
1 cup all-purpose flour
1 cup water
1 teaspoon baking powder
½ teaspoon salt
2 tablespoons vegetable oil

Slice the zucchini into ½" coins. In a large bowl, whisk together the flour, water, baking powder, and salt until blended though still lumpy. Fold in the zucchini until evenly coated.

In a large skillet, heat the oil over medium-high heat. Test with a few drops of batter. The oil is ready when the batter immediately bubbles and sets.

Working in batches, fry the zucchini coins 3–4 minutes on each side until crispy and golden brown. Space the coins far enough apart so they do not touch.

Drain on paper towels and let cool. Refrigerate leftovers and reheat them in a toaster oven.

Makes about 3 cups

Vegetable Fritters

1 cup all-purpose flour
1 cup water
1 teaspoon baking powder
½ teaspoon salt
2 cups julienned vegetables, such as carrots, zucchini, onion, green peppers, or eggplant
2 tablespoons vegetable oil

In a large bowl, whisk together the flour, water, baking powder, and salt until blended though still lumpy. Fold in the vegetables, stirring until evenly coated. In a large skillet, heat the oil over medium-high heat. Drop ½ cup of the fritter mixture into the skillet for each fritter. Use the back of a spoon to slightly flatten each fritter. Cook 4–5 minutes on each side, or until golden brown. Drain on paper towels and let cool. Refrigerate leftovers and reheat them in a toaster oven.

Makes about 10 fritters

CHAPTER 5

BREAKFAST AND BRUNCH

The morning rush at any household with children is a lesson in controlled chaos. Your child is ready to go as soon as he wakes up and doesn't care when you wake up, have your coffee, or go to work. Finding time in the mornings to cook is a real challenge, so keep things simple and quick. On the plus side, I do find that most children like to eat the same two or three things for breakfast every day. So if you can find these reliable standbys, then your mornings might find a manageable rhythm.

Alexei's breakfast for the past year has consisted of diluted orange juice, a bowl of cereal (raisin bran or toasted O's), a small banana, and either two slices of raisin bread with a little peanut butter or two slices of French toast. It took many bowls of rejected oatmeal to come to this happy consensus. On weekends, when I have more time, I often make pancakes or waffles as a treat. Omelets and egg dishes have actually become favorite lunches. Ask your pediatrician about when and how to introduce eggs into your baby's diet.

In this chapter...

RICE CEREAL

Your baby's first cereal doesn't have to come from a box. Make the rice, then stir in prepared formula or breast milk to fortify it when you are ready to feed your child.

> 1 cup rice
> 2 cups water
>   Prepared infant formula or breast milk

In a medium saucepan, bring the rice and water to a boil over high heat. Reduce the heat to low, cover, and simmer for 15 minutes or until the rice is tender. This will look soupy, or like tapioca with the rice in a milky liquid. Uncover and let cool in the pan.

In batches, puree in a blender or food mill. Stir up to ¼ cup of formula or breast milk into each serving to achieve a texture appropriate for your infant.

Makes about 2 cups

WHOLE WHEAT WAFFLES

Now is the time to haul out those wedding gifts, like waffle irons and food processors, that have been collecting dust in the cupboards.

> 1 cup whole wheat flour
> ½ cup all-purpose flour
> 2 teaspoons baking powder
> ½ teaspoon salt
> 2 eggs
> 1½ cups milk
> 3 tablespoons vegetable oil
> Maple syrup or powdered sugar

In a large bowl, stir together the whole wheat flour, all-purpose flour, baking powder, and salt with a fork until combined. Stir in the eggs, milk, and oil until blended. Pour the batter into your hot, seasoned waffle iron and cook according to the manufacturer's instructions.

Serve with maple syrup or powdered sugar.

Makes about 12 (4") waffles

BISTRO BITS: These waffles freeze well. Simply cool completely, then place in a food storage bag and freeze for up to 2 months.

WHOLE WHEAT PANCAKES

This is a denser pancake, full of flavor and texture. A good recipe for making smaller, "mouse ears" pancakes.

1 cup whole wheat flour
½ cup all-purpose flour
2 teaspoons baking powder
½ teaspoon baking soda
½ teaspoon salt
1 egg
½ cup milk
½ cup plain yogurt
4 tablespoons vegetable oil
2 tablespoons honey
½ cup chopped pecans or walnuts (optional)
Maple syrup or powdered sugar

In a large bowl, stir together the whole wheat flour, all-purpose flour, baking powder, baking soda, and salt with a fork until combined. Stir in the egg, milk, yogurt, 2 tablespoons of the oil, and the honey until blended though still lumpy. Stir in the pecans or walnuts, if using.

In a large skillet, heat the remaining 2 tablespoons oil over medium heat. Pour the batter by ¼ cupfuls into the skillet. Cook until the bottom is golden brown and the top is covered with bubbles. Turn the pancakes and cook for 1–2 minutes or until done. Serve with maple syrup or powdered sugar.

Makes 12 (4") pancakes

BLUEBERRY PANCAKES

This is a classic buttermilk pancake recipe made with yogurt instead of buttermilk. I was delighted to learn that the two are often interchangeable since we usually have yogurt in the fridge, but a Sunday morning trip to the store for buttermilk would be unheard of in our house.

1   cup all-purpose flour
1   teaspoon baking powder
½   teaspoon baking soda
½   teaspoon salt
1   egg
1   cup plain yogurt
4   tablespoons vegetable oil
½   cup fresh or frozen thawed blueberries
    Maple syrup or powdered sugar

In a large bowl, stir together the flour, baking powder, baking soda, and salt with a fork until combined. Stir in the egg, yogurt, and 2 tablespoons of the oil until blended though still lumpy. Gently fold in the blueberries.

In a large skillet, heat the remaining 2 tablespoons oil over medium heat. Pour the batter by ¼ cupfuls into the skillet. Cook until the bottom is golden brown and the top is covered with bubbles. Turn the pancakes and cook for 1–2 minutes or until done. Serve with maple syrup or powdered sugar.

Makes about 10 (4") pancakes

PUFFY APPLE PANCAKE

Use apples, apricots, peaches, or whatever firm fruit you have on hand.
This is a wonderful treat for a big family brunch or sleepover breakfast.

2 tablespoons butter
2 large apples, peeled, cored, and sliced
2 tablespoons sugar
1 teaspoon ground cinnamon
3 eggs
½ cup all-purpose flour
½ cup milk
¼ cup plain yogurt
½ teaspoon salt

Preheat the oven to 375°F.

In a large ovenproof skillet, melt the butter over medium-
high heat. Add the apples and cook, stirring occasionally,
for 5 minutes or until tender. Sprinkle the sugar and cinnamon over the apples and set aside.

In a medium bowl, whisk the eggs until slightly foamy, then
stir in the flour, milk, yogurt, and salt until blended and
smooth. Pour the batter over the apples and bake for
20–30 minutes or until lightly golden and puffy. Remove
from the oven and let cool slightly. To serve, cut into 8
wedges.

Makes 8 wedges

BISTRO BITS: If your skillet has a handle that is not ovenproof, thoroughly wrap the handle with aluminum foil.

FREEZING BREAKFAST FOODS

Many breakfast foods freeze beautifully. Waffles, pancakes, and even French toast make a convenient, healthful fast food when your homemade version is pulled from the oven. Simply cook as directed and then cool completely. Place in a food storage bag and freeze for up to 2 months. To use, remove from the freezer and toast in a toaster or toaster oven.

FRENCH TOAST FINGERS

I started making these for Alexei when he was in his anti-egg, anti-meat, anti-spoon, anti-nearly-everything phase. Thankfully, these are high in protein and with just a little sugar, a reliably yummy breakfast.

1 egg
¼ cup milk
¼ teaspoon vanilla extract
½ teaspoon ground cinnamon
1 tablespoon butter
2 slices enriched white bread or challah
Powdered sugar

In a medium bowl, whisk together the egg, milk, vanilla, and cinnamon until blended and smooth. In a large skillet, melt the butter over medium heat. Dip each side of the bread slices into the egg mixture. When the butter foams, add the slices to the pan.

Cook until the bottom is golden brown. Turn the bread slices and cook for 2 minutes longer or until done.

To serve, sprinkle with powdered sugar and slice each into 4 "fingers."

Makes 8 fingers

BISTRO BITS: It is very important to thoroughly cook the egg within the bread to avoid the risk of salmonella poisoning. However, French toast browns very quickly, so keep the heat no hotter than medium.

BLUEBERRY MUFFINS

This recipe works with any fruit. Cranberries are a delicious alternative to blueberries, and I often mix the two.

2 cups all-purpose flour
¼ cup packed brown sugar
2 teaspoons baking powder
½ teaspoon salt
1 egg
½ cup milk
½ cup plain yogurt
2 tablespoons vegetable oil
1 cup fresh or frozen thawed blueberries

Preheat the oven to 350°F. Grease a 12-cup muffin pan; set aside.

In a large bowl, stir together the flour, brown sugar, baking powder, and salt with a fork until combined. Stir in the egg, milk, yogurt, and oil until just until blended. Fold in the blueberries.

Fill each muffin cup about ⅔ full. Bake for 15–20 minutes or until a toothpick inserted in the center comes out clean. Remove from the oven and cool on a wire rack for 5 minutes. Remove from the pan and cool completely on the rack.

Makes 12 muffins

BANANA BREAD

Everybody's favorite quick bread is also the savior of many a banana in our house.

3 very ripe bananas, peeled and mashed with a fork
1 egg
½ cup packed brown sugar
¼ cup vegetable oil
1 teaspoon vanilla extract
1½ cups all-purpose flour
2 teaspoons baking powder
½ teaspoon baking soda
1 teaspoon ground cinnamon

Preheat the oven to 350°F. Grease a 9" × 5" loaf pan; set aside.

In a large bowl, whisk together the bananas, egg, brown sugar, oil, and vanilla just until blended. Add the flour, baking powder, baking soda, and cinnamon and stir just until blended. Pour into the prepared pan and bake for 45–55 minutes or until a toothpick inserted in the center comes out clean.

Remove from the oven and cool for 10 minutes on a wire rack. Remove the bread from the pan and let cool completely on the rack. To serve, cut into 12 slices.

Makes 12 slices

CRANBERRY BREAD

2 cups all-purpose flour
½ cup packed brown sugar
2 teaspoons baking powder
½ teaspoon baking soda
½ teaspoon salt
1 egg
½ cup orange juice
2 tablespoons vegetable oil
1 cup fresh or frozen thawed cranberries

Preheat the oven to 350°F. Grease a 9" × 5" loaf pan; set aside.

In a large bowl, stir together the flour, brown sugar, baking powder, baking soda, and salt with a fork until combined. Stir in the egg, orange juice, and oil just until blended. Fold in the cranberries. Pour into the prepared pan and bake for 50–60 minutes or until a toothpick inserted in the center comes out clean.

Remove from the oven and cool for 10 minutes on a wire rack. Remove the bread from the pan and cool completely on the rack. To serve, cut into 12 slices.

Makes 12 slices

BISTRO BITS: This bread freezes quite well. I slice the bread and wrap each slice in waxed or parchment paper, then put these wrapped slices in a plastic storage bag. This makes for convenient defrosting later.

BREAKFAST CAKE

This is really just a simple coffee cake recipe with the sugar reduced, but it is very easy to whip up (under 45 minutes including baking time) and delicious.

Cake

1½ cups all-purpose flour
½ cup packed brown sugar
2 teaspoons baking powder
1 teaspoon baking soda
½ teaspoon salt
2 eggs
1 cup sour cream

Streusel Topping

3 tablespoons all-purpose flour
3 tablespoons packed brown sugar
2 tablespoons butter
½ teaspoon ground cinnamon
¼ cup chopped pecans (optional)

Preheat the oven to 350°F. Grease a 9" × 9" square baking pan; set aside.

To make the cake: In a large bowl, stir together the flour, brown sugar, baking powder, baking soda, and salt with a fork until combined. In a medium bowl, whisk together the eggs and sour cream until smooth and a lemony color. Stir the egg mixture into the dry ingredients just until blended and smooth. Spread evenly into the prepared pan.

To make the streusel topping: In a medium bowl, using a pastry blender or 2 knives in scissors fashion, combine the flour, brown sugar, butter, and cinnamon until well-blended and crumbly. Stir in the pecans, if using. Sprinkle the topping over the cake and bake for 15–20 minutes or until a toothpick inserted in the center comes out clean. Remove from the oven and let cool on a wire rack. To serve, cut into 16 squares.

Makes 16 squares

Fresh Mozzarella Omelet

Alexei went through a stage of only eating with his hands. So even eggs had to become finger food. Fresh mozzarella is great for this recipe as it retains its tender yet firm texture.

1 egg
¼ cup milk
1 tablespoon butter
2 thin slices fresh mozzarella cheese

In a medium bowl, whisk together the egg and milk until blended and smooth. In a medium skillet, melt the butter over medium heat. When the butter foams, add the egg mixture. Cook until the egg is just set.

Place the mozzarella slices down the center third of the omelet. Carefully fold the sides of the omelet over the mozzarella. Cook just 1 minute longer to warm the cheese.

To serve, cut crosswise into slices for finger food or smaller bites to spoon feed.

Makes 1 omelet

BISTRO BITS: This recipe, like most egg dishes, does not freeze well. It does, however, cook up in a flash.

Steamed Japanese Egg Custard

Smooth and delectably mild, this was a favorite of my childhood. It really does steam up like a custard. This does not freeze well, but it does keep well in the refrigerator for a day or two. Leftovers make a balanced lunch mixed into rice and grated cheese.

1   egg
½   cup water
    Salt to taste

In a 6-ounce custard cup or ramekin, whisk together the egg and water until blended and smooth. Season with salt and any add-ins (see note below).

Put a steamer basket in a medium saucepan with 1" water. Carefully place the custard cup in the steamer basket. Cover and bring to a boil over medium-high heat. Reduce the heat to medium and steam for 10–12 minutes or until the custard is set and a knife inserted in the center comes out clean.

Makes 1 custard

BISTRO BITS: As your child's tastes change, you can add in any of the following to liven up the flavor of this dish.

- 1 finely chopped scallion
- ½ tablespoon chopped parsley, basil, or any other fresh herb
- Chopped roasted red peppers or tomatoes
- Sprinkle of sweet paprika

Spinach and Goat Cheese Scramble

Think goat cheese sounds too sophisticated? Many babies find its mild, tangy flavor delectable. If not the case for your baby, try fresh mozzarella.

1 egg
3 tablespoons milk
1 tablespoon butter
½ cup torn fresh spinach leaves
2 tablespoons crumbled mild goat cheese

In a medium bowl, whisk together the egg and milk until blended and smooth. In a medium skillet, melt the butter over medium heat. When the butter foams, add the egg mixture.

Reduce the heat to low. With a spatula, stir up the egg as it sets until fluffy and almost cooked. Stir in the spinach.

The spinach will quickly wilt and brighten in color. Stir in the goat cheese. Serve immediately.

Makes 1 scramble

EASY FRITTATA

1 tablespoon butter or vegetable oil
½ small onion, sliced
6 eggs, beaten
1 small tomato, seeded and diced
1 sliced, boiled potato (leftover is great; peel for infants)
½ teaspoon salt (optional)

Preheat the oven to 350°F.

In a large ovenproof skillet (see note below), heat the butter or oil over medium heat. Add the onion and cook, stirring occasionally, for 5 minutes or until tender. Stir in the eggs, tomato, potato, and salt, if using. Reduce the heat to low and cook until the bottoms of the eggs are set, about 5 minutes. Place the skillet in the oven and bake for 10 minutes or until lightly puffed and set in the center. To serve, cut into 6 wedges.

Makes 6 wedges

BISTRO BITS: If your skillet has a handle that is not ovenproof, thoroughly wrap the handle with aluminum foil.

BREAKFAST BURRITO

Made with a taco-size tortilla, this petite burrito is a great breakfast on the go.

> 1 egg
> ¼ cup milk
> 1 tablespoon olive oil
> 1 flour tortilla (7"–8")

In a medium bowl, whisk together the egg and milk until blended and smooth. In a medium skillet, heat the oil over medium heat. Add the egg mixture. Reduce the heat to low and cook, stirring with a spatula, until the egg is fluffy and cooked through.

Meanwhile, microwave the tortilla for about 5 seconds or until hot. Spoon the eggs onto the center third of the tortilla. Add any toppings (see note on the opposite page). Fold the "long" ends toward the center first, then roll, starting with a short end, into a neat bundle. Serve warm. To hold a burrito together while on the go, simply wrap in aluminum foil or parchment paper.

Makes 1 burrito

BISTRO BITS: Add any of these toppings to the eggs before you roll up the burrito.

- Shredded Cheddar cheese

- Finely chopped scallion

- Diced tomato

- Mild salsa

EGG SUBSTITUTES

If your child is allergic to eggs, I can't enthusiastically recommend the available egg substitutes. They just don't taste very good. Moreover, they are actually egg whites and were created for cholesterol-conscious diets, not for those with allergies. Speak with your doctor about these substitutes. A nice alternative, if your child can eat soy, would be to "scramble" silken-textured tofu with spinach and goat cheese. It's still an easy, delicious way to serve protein.

HASH BROWN PATTIES

2 large potatoes, unpeeled
1 small onion, minced
2 tablespoons vegetable oil

Using a box grater or food processor, coarsely grate the potatoes. In a large bowl, combine the potatoes and onion. In a large nonstick skillet, heat 1 tablespoon of the oil over medium-high heat. Evenly divide the mixture into 8 portions. Place 4 of the portions in the pan, flattening them with the back of the spoon. Each hash brown patty should be about 3" wide and no more than ¾" thick. Cook for 10 minutes or until the bottom is browned and crispy. Turn the patties and cook for 10 minutes or until each patty is cooked through. Repeat with the remaining oil and potato portions.

Makes 8 patties

VEGETARIAN HASH

Make this as spicy as your child likes. It is best topped with a fried egg.

2 tablespoons vegetable oil
½ small onion, diced
¼ cup finely chopped red bell pepper
1 cup diced, cooked potato (a leftover baked or boiled potato is fine)
½ cup frozen thawed corn kernels (leftover corn off the cob is even better)
2 tablespoons tamari sauce
¼ teaspoon sweet paprika
Cayenne pepper to taste (optional)

In a medium skillet, heat the oil over medium-high heat. Add the onion and red pepper and cook, stirring occasionally, for 3 minutes. Stir in the potato, corn, tamari, paprika, and cayenne pepper, if using. Cook, stirring constantly, making sure the hash doesn't scorch on the bottom, until the potatoes are browned and slightly crisp.

Makes about 2 cups

CHAPTER 6

LUNCH AND DINNER

Parents love to announce milestones in their child's food reper-
toire. "He ate chicken for the first time!" "She picked up her own noodles!" We've all bored our nonparent friends with overly detailed
accounts of our children's meals. It's exciting to us! Watching your child
eat "people food," as our pediatrician calls it, is very endearing and at the
same time can be fiercely frustrating, so these small victories mean a great
deal to earnest parents. The best way to expand your child's palate is to
constantly introduce new dishes while not intimidating him with too many
new tastes too fast. We often let Alexei taste what we're eating for dinner,
either at home or out, and if he seems interested, I'll try making it for him.
This is how many of these recipes came about.

Don't slave for hours making gallons of chicken chili unless your child
has tried it, or something like it, and seemed interested. Alexei will often
explore a new food with his fingers and nose before he even puts it any-
where near his mouth. This get-to-know-you phase can last as many as 10
attempts with a new dish. I think he is still rather dubious about edamame.

In this chapter...

CHEESE QUESADILLAS

½ teaspoon vegetable oil (or a light spray)
2 corn or flour tortillas (8" each)
½ cup shredded Cheddar cheese
1 scallion, chopped (optional)
2 slices tomato (optional)

In a large skillet, heat the oil over medium heat. Place 1 tortilla in the pan and heat for 15 seconds. Turn the tortilla over and sprinkle with the cheese, scallion (if using), and tomato (if using). Lay the second tortilla on top and press down. Using a wide spatula and a fork, carefully flip the quesadilla over and cook for 1 minute or until the cheese melts. You will spill some cheese or toppings while flipping, and that is to be expected. Cut into 4 quarters.

Makes 4 quarters

TOASTED CHEESE SANDWICH

Of course you know how to make a toasted cheese sandwich. But even a 1-year-old can tire of his usual favorite. For 2 weeks straight, Alexei would eat nothing *but* toasted cheese sandwiches, and then even he finally threw one down in protest. Try these twists on the traditional American cheese on white bread.

Breads

Marbled rye
Whole grain
Thinly sliced French
Pita
Focaccia sliced in half
Raisin

Cheeses

Swiss
Sharp Cheddar
Mild goat
Smoked Gouda
Brie

Put 2 bread slices on a cutting board. Place or spread some cheese on one slice. Put both slices in a toaster oven and toast just until the cheese starts to melt. Put the slices together.

Take a cookie cutter and create fun shapes for your child. Hearts, stars, animals, whatever, are captivating to hold and eat.

Or slice each sandwich into 4 rectangles, squares, or triangles for easy finger food.

Makes 1 sandwich

BISTRO BITS: These are great for traveling. I make two before we get on the road, cut them up into triangles, and pack them in an insulated bag for easy-to-reach snacking and meals.

Tea Sandwiches

These very ladylike sandwiches are perfect for birthday parties or when you might be hosting a playgroup. The key is to spread the filling evenly and lightly between the bread.

2 slices white, whole wheat, or raisin bread

¼ cup No-Mayo Tuna Salad (opposite page), Honey-Walnut Cream Cheese (opposite page), or No-Mayo Egg Salad (page 88) fillings

Evenly spread 1 slice of bread with the filling. Top with the other slice of bread and cut into 4 triangles.

Makes 4 triangles

No-Mayo Tuna Salad

2 tablespoons olive oil
1 tablespoon Dijon mustard
1 tablespoon red wine vinegar
1 can (6 ounces) solid white tuna packed in water, flaked
2 baby carrots, diced
½ rib celery, diced

In a medium bowl, whisk together the oil, mustard, and vinegar. Add the tuna, carrots, and celery and toss to coat well.

Makes about 1½ cups

Honey-Walnut Cream Cheese

½ cup cream cheese, softened
¼ cup chopped walnuts
2 tablespoons honey

In a medium bowl, using a rubber spatula, stir together the cream cheese, walnuts, and honey until blended.

Makes ¾ cup

NO-MAYO EGG SALAD

2 eggs
2 tablespoons olive oil
1 tablespoon red wine vinegar
1 teaspoon chopped chives (optional)
Sweet paprika (optional)

Put eggs in a small saucepan with enough water to cover by 1". Bring to a boil over high heat. Reduce the heat to low and simmer for 10 minutes.

Immediately remove the eggs to a colander and rinse with cold water until cool. Peel the eggs. Slice the eggs in half and remove the yolks.

Place the yolks in a small bowl. Add the oil, vinegar, and chives, if using, and mix until smooth and creamy. Dice the egg whites and fold into the yolk mixture. Sprinkle with paprika, if using.

Makes about ¾ cup

MINI BURGERS

I've taken these to potluck lunches with great success, although it's quite often the parents who are scrambling for these cute little burgers.

1 pound ground beef
8 Parker House rolls, or any small dinner roll
  Ketchup, mustard, or other condiments

Preheat the grill or broiler. Shape the ground beef into 8 small patties. I use an ice cream scoop. Each scoop yields an even portion, and then I gently flatten each ball into a patty. Grill over medium heat or broil for 4 minutes on each side or until thoroughly cooked and no longer pink.

Serve each patty in a split roll with ketchup, mustard, and other condiments on the side.

Makes about 8 burgers

Turkey Burgers

I usually buy ground dark or thigh meat, as it's tastier and juicier than ground white meat.

1	pound ground turkey
½	cup bread crumbs
½	small onion, minced
½	cup milk
½	teaspoon sweet paprika

Preheat the grill or broiler.

In a large bowl, mix the turkey, bread crumbs, onion, milk, and paprika just until thoroughly combined. Shape into 8 small patties (see Mini Burgers recipe, page 89).

Grill over medium heat or broil for 4 minutes on each side or until thoroughly cooked and no longer pink.

Serve with split buns or cut into small pieces for beginning eaters.

Makes about 8 burgers

LENTIL BURGERS

This is a good recipe for leftover lentils and rice, both of which beautifully absorb spices and flavorings.

1 cup cooked lentils
½ cup cooked brown rice
½ small onion, diced
1 baby carrot, minced
1 egg
½ teaspoon sweet paprika
Salt to taste
Ground black pepper to taste
2 tablespoons vegetable oil

In a large bowl, mix the lentils, rice, onion, carrot, egg, paprika, salt, and pepper until thoroughly combined. The mixture should loosely hold together.

In a large skillet, heat the oil over medium heat. Use a ½-cup measure or large spoon to scoop six ½-cup portions of the lentil mixture into the hot skillet. Cook for 5–10 minutes or until the bottom is set and golden brown. With a spatula, gently turn and cook for 5–10 minutes or until set and golden brown on the other side.

Serve like hamburgers on buns or cut into small pieces.

Makes about 6 burgers

Turkey and Apple Sausage Patties

These patties are great finger food—firm enough to hold with tiny hands, but tender and crumbly for easier chewing. Nothing was more unappetizing to Alexei than plain turkey, so I added applesauce, chopped spinach (just because I could sneak it in), and lots of sage and celery for a very mild sausage patty.

1 tablespoon olive oil
1 cup torn fresh spinach
1 small onion, chopped
1 rib celery, chopped
1 pound ground turkey thigh (ground breast is too dry)
¾ cup unsweetened applesauce
1 teaspoon dried sage leaves

In a large skillet, heat the oil over medium-high heat. Add the spinach and cook, quickly working the spinach down with tongs or a wooden spoon, until wilted but still bright green. Remove the spinach to a plate and cool.

Reduce the heat to medium. In the same skillet, add the onion and celery and cook, stirring occasionally, for 10 minutes or until tender.

Coarsely chop the cooked spinach. In a large bowl, mix the spinach, onion, celery, turkey, applesauce, and sage just until well-blended.

Shape into twenty-five 2" patties, each about 1" thick. Heat a large nonstick skillet over medium heat. In batches, cook the patties for 5 minutes on each side or until thoroughly cooked and no longer pink.

Makes about 25 patties

BISTRO BITS: These freeze extremely well, especially if you wrap them individually in plastic wrap. Otherwise, thoroughly cool them to room temperature and freeze 5 or 10 in a sealed plastic storage bag.

Chicken Nuggets

No matter how hard parents try, nothing seems as tasty to a kid as those ubiquitous chicken nuggets. After many attempts and eating far too many fast-food nuggets in the name of research, I realized that the appeal lies in their salty taste and their texture. Or rather, their lack of texture. Then it all seemed simple—ground chicken with a lightly seasoned breading.

1 cup bread crumbs
⅛–¼ teaspoon salt
¼ teaspoon sweet paprika (optional)
1 pound ground chicken
2 tablespoons vegetable oil

Preheat the oven to 200°F.

In a deep bowl, mix the bread crumbs, salt, and paprika, if using. With your hands, shape the chicken into thirty 2"–3" nuggets. Toss the nuggets in the bread-crumb mixture until evenly coated.

In a large skillet, heat the oil over medium heat. In batches, cook the nuggets for 3 minutes on each side until golden, crispy, and thoroughly cooked. You can keep cooked nuggets warm in the oven while you finish.

Makes about 30 nuggets

FALAFEL

This is nothing like the deep-fried balls bought from a street cart. I've found that the easiest falafel recipe is just a modified version of hummus—beans, spices, lemon, and olive oil. This fries to a nice crispiness even without a lot of oil. You can omit the tahini if your child is allergic to sesame.

1   can (14 ounces) chickpeas
1   small clove garlic, chopped
½   small onion, chopped
2   tablespoons tahini (or substitute ¼ teaspoon sea salt)
    Juice of ½ lemon
    Salt to taste (no more than ½ teaspoon)
3   tablespoons olive oil

In a blender or food processor, puree the chickpeas, garlic, onion, tahini, lemon juice, salt, and 1 tablespoon of the oil. The mixture should have the thick, somewhat stiff consistency of peanut butter.

In a large skillet, heat the remaining 2 tablespoons oil over medium heat. Drop tablespoons of the chickpea mixture into the pan and cook for 5 minutes or until golden brown on the bottom. Turn and cook for 3–5 minutes or until golden brown on the other side.

Makes about 20 patties

Spinach Pie

Alexei loves those little stuffed phyllo hors d'oeuvres at cocktail parties, but a larger pie seemed a more reasonable workweek compromise.

4	tablespoons olive oil
½	small onion, minced
1	clove garlic, minced
1	pound fresh spinach
1	egg
6	sheets phyllo dough, thawed and cut in half lengthwise

Preheat the oven to 350°F. Lightly oil a 9" pie plate.

In a large skillet, heat 1 tablespoon oil over medium-high heat and cook the onion and garlic, stirring occasionally, for 5 minutes or until tender. Add the spinach in handfuls and cook, quickly working the spinach down with tongs or a wooden spoon, until wilted but still bright green. Remove from the heat and let cool.

Using your hands, squeeze out any excess moisture from the spinach mixture and then chop.

In a medium bowl, combine the spinach mixture and egg until blended.

Arrange ½ sheet of the phyllo in the pie plate, letting the excess hang over the edges. Lightly brush with some of the oil and repeat with 5 more ½ sheets, evenly covering the bottom of the pan. Evenly spread the spinach mixture over the phyllo. Arrange ½ sheet of the phyllo on top of the spinach mixture, letting the excess hang over the edges. Lightly brush this sheet with some of the oil and repeat with the remaining 5 more ½ sheets, evenly covering the top of the pie. Finish with a last light brush of oil and tuck in any overhanging pieces of phyllo.

Bake for 30 minutes or until the phyllo is lightly golden in the center and beginning to brown around the edges. Cool and slice into 8 wedges or smaller bites.

Makes 8 wedges

CHICKEN AND WHITE BEAN CHILI

Chicken, beans, tomatoes, corn—this is as healthy as it is delicious. It's also one of those meals that you can easily adapt to your child's ever-changing diet. Add more spice when he's ready. Or leave out the chili powder, keep everything chunky, and let him eat it with his hands.

    1 tablespoon olive oil
    ½ pound ground chicken
    1 small onion, diced
    ½ red bell pepper, diced
    1 can (14 ounces) white beans (cannellini, navy, great Northern), rinsed and drained
    1 can (14 ounces) crushed tomatoes
    ½ cup frozen thawed or fresh corn kernels
  ⅛–¼ teaspoon chili powder (optional)

In a large nonstick skillet, heat the oil over medium-high heat and cook the ground chicken, crumbling it with a spoon until browned. Add the onion and red pepper and cook, stirring occasionally, for 10 minutes or until the vegetables are tender. Add the white beans, tomatoes, corn, and chili powder, if using. Bring to a simmer.

Reduce the heat to medium-low. Cover and simmer for 15 minutes. Serve as is or process to a consistency appropriate for your child.

Makes 6 cups

BISTRO BITS: This recipe doubles and triples very easily and freezes quite well in ice cube trays or small plastic storage containers.

Does your child love spicy food? A lot of children do. Our friend Jack even eats those wicked little peppers at Chinese restaurants. Keep a few things in mind.

- Add in chili powder, chopped jalapeño peppers, or ground black pepper at your discretion, but always start with small amounts.

- Keep in mind that fresh peppers mellow out with longer cooking.

- Don't add spicy peppers if your child will be eating this with his hands. His eyes will tear up with pain if he touches his fingers to his eyes.

Black Bean Soup

1 tablespoon olive oil
1 small onion, minced
1 can (14 ounces) black beans, rinsed and drained
1 can (14 ounces) low-sodium chicken broth
1 cup water
½ cup diced leftover cooked ham, pork roast, or beef

In a medium saucepan, heat the oil over medium-high heat and cook the onion, stirring occasionally, for 5 minutes or until tender.

Add the black beans; chicken broth; water; and ham, pork roast, or beef and bring to a boil over high heat. Reduce the heat to low, cover, and simmer for about 30 minutes.

Serve as is, or puree in batches for younger palates.

Makes about 3 cups

LEMON AND RICE SOUP

This is the classic Greek avgolemono soup that I adore. It's a refreshing, light chicken broth and rice soup enlivened with lemon juice.

1 can (14 ounces) low-sodium chicken broth
½ cup cooked rice
Juice of 1 lemon
1 egg

In a medium saucepan, bring the broth to a boil over medium-high heat. Stir in the rice and lemon juice. Crack the egg into a measuring cup or small bowl and while whisking the egg, slowly add about ½ cup of broth. Gently stir the egg mixture back into the saucepan, creating thin cooked ribbons of egg throughout the broth.

Makes about 3 cups

Corn Chowder

Another recipe inspired by our summers in New England. Add diced carrots or squash to it for color if you like.

1 tablespoon butter
1 tablespoon all-purpose flour
1 cup milk
1 cup low-sodium chicken broth
1 small potato, peeled and diced
1 cup frozen thawed or fresh corn kernels

In a medium saucepan, melt the butter over medium heat. Reduce the heat to low, add the flour, and cook, stirring constantly, for 2 minutes or until the mixture is bubbly and golden. Whisk in the milk and cook, stirring frequently, for 10 minutes or until the milk thickens. Add the broth, potato, and corn and simmer, stirring occasionally, for 15 minutes or until the potato is tender.

Serve as is to older toddlers or puree for younger tots and beginning eaters.

Makes about 3 cups

CHICKEN AND VEGETABLE SOUP

Once I started making fresh soups, canned varieties all tasted terribly "canned." If you're pressed for time, use high-quality frozen mixed vegetables.

1 can (14 ounces) low-sodium chicken broth
1 cup water
1 cup chopped leftover boneless chicken
1 carrot, chopped
1 rib celery, chopped
½ cup green beans, cut into ½" pieces
¼ cup tiny pasta (stars, alphabet, or orzo)

In a medium saucepan, bring the broth and water to a boil over high heat. Add the chicken, carrot, celery, green beans, and pasta. Reduce the heat to low and simmer, stirring occasionally, for 10 minutes or until the pasta is cooked.

Serve as is to older toddlers or puree for younger tots and beginning eaters.

Makes about 4 cups

SEAFOOD BISQUE

I've noticed that many kids go through a love-hate relationship with fish. Sometimes it is too "fishy." This soup is a tasty, though mild, way of serving your favorite seafood.

> 1 tablespoon butter
> 1 tablespoon all-purpose flour
> 1 cup milk
> 1 can (14 ounces) low-sodium chicken broth
> 2 tablespoons tomato paste
> ¾ cup cubed seafood, such as sea bass, cod, shrimp, scallops, or lobster

In a medium saucepan, melt the butter over medium heat. Reduce the heat to low, add the flour, and cook, stirring constantly, for 2 minutes or until the mixture is bubbly and golden. Whisk in the milk and cook, stirring frequently, for 10 minutes or until the milk thickens. Stir in the broth and tomato paste until it is an even pink color.

Add the seafood and simmer for 5 minutes or until the seafood is thoroughly cooked. Let the soup cool slightly in the pot. In batches, puree in a blender or food processor.

Makes about 3 cups

Butternut Squash Soup

This is a family favorite, especially on a cold day.

1 butternut squash
1 small onion, chopped
1 can (14 ounces) low-sodium chicken broth
1 tablespoon minced gingerroot
1 teaspoon ground cinnamon
1 cup milk

Peel the squash, slice it in half, and remove the pulp and seeds. Chop into 2" pieces.

In a large saucepan, bring the chopped squash, onion, broth, ginger, and cinnamon to a boil over high heat. Reduce the heat to low, cover, and simmer for 30 minutes or until the squash is tender. Let the soup cool slightly in the pot.

In batches, puree in a blender or food processor, returning the puree to the pot. Over low heat, stir in the milk and heat through.

Makes about 6 cups

RATATOUILLE

With sincere apologies to the Mmes. Child, Bertholle, and Beck, whose *Mastering the Art of French Cooking* inspired this simply delicious, healthy recipe that tastes even better the next day.

1 small eggplant
1 tablespoon salt
2 tablespoons olive oil
1 zucchini, thinly sliced
1 small green bell pepper, thinly sliced
1 small onion, thinly sliced
1 clove garlic, crushed
1 can (14 ounces) crushed tomatoes
1 bay leaf
Cooked rice (optional)

Cut the eggplant into 1"-thick slices. In a colander, toss the eggplant with the salt and let rest for 30 minutes. The bitter, dark juices of the eggplant will be drawn out. Rinse the salt off the eggplant.

In a large saucepan, heat the oil over medium-high heat and in batches, brown the eggplant. It is important to cook the eggplant slices in small batches so that they brown properly. Once all of the eggplant is browned, remove to a dish.

In the same pan, add the zucchini and cook, stirring occasionally, for 5 minutes or until golden. Add the pepper, onion, and garlic and cook, stirring occasionally, for 10 minutes or until the onion is soft and translucent. Return the eggplant to the pan. Stir in the tomatoes and bay leaf. Bring to a boil over high heat. Reduce the heat to low, cover, and simmer for at least 30 minutes to blend flavors.

Cool slightly and remove and discard the bay leaf. Serve as is or puree in a food processor or blender to a consistency appropriate for your child.

Serve, if desired, over hot cooked rice.

Makes 5 cups

BISTRO BITS: You can use the long, thin Japanese eggplant in place of the typical Italian eggplant and skip the salting method. It is a little more difficult to find but has a milder, sweeter flavor.

What a lot of ratatouille! The flavor of this earthy dish deepens over a day or two and it freezes well. Keep 3–4 days' worth in the fridge and freeze the rest. Or try these options.

- The classic French way to serve ratatouille is with lamb. Add finely chopped leftover lamb or roast beef.

- Puree into a hearty soup. Top with a sprinkle of Parmesan cheese.

- Serve on top of sautéed fish or scrambled tofu.

Risotto

Don't reach for your truffle shaver—yet. This is the simplest risotto recipe that uses the starch of the rice rather than broth and butter for its rich, creamy consistency.

½ cup short-grain rice
1½ cups low-sodium chicken broth
½ cup frozen thawed baby peas
½ cup shredded cooked chicken
1–2 tablespoons grated Parmesan cheese

In a medium saucepan, bring the rice and broth to a boil over high heat and continue boiling, stirring occasionally, for 10 minutes. Reduce the heat to medium and stir in the peas and chicken. Cover and cook for 15 minutes or until the rice has absorbed most of the liquid. Stir in the cheese and let cool slightly. Serve as is or puree in a food processor or blender to a consistency appropriate for your child.

Makes 3 cups

BISTRO BITS: You can freeze this dish in an ice cube tray or small freezer-safe storage containers. The texture of the rice will be slightly gummy upon its defrosting, but it's easily fixed with a pat of butter or a splash of milk.

FIRST FRIED RICE

1 tablespoon vegetable oil
2 scallions, finely chopped
2 baby carrots, diced
1 cup cooked brown rice
½ cup frozen thawed peas
1 tablespoon low-sodium soy sauce
1 egg

In a large skillet, heat the oil over medium heat. Add the scallions and carrots and cook, stirring occasionally, for 3 minutes or until tender. Stir in the rice, breaking up any clumps. Stir in the peas and soy sauce and cook, stirring, until evenly coated and heated through.

Push the rice mixture to the outer edges of the skillet and crack the egg into the center. Break the yolk with a spatula and cook with short, quick strokes, as if making scrambled eggs. Once the egg is set, stir into the rice and serve.

Makes about 2 cups

RICE AND ORZO PILAF

Alexei gobbles up this simple dish, and so does his dad! Since we eat it so often ourselves, it makes for reliable leftovers to keep in the refrigerator.

1 tablespoon butter
1 cup rice
½ cup orzo pasta (or any tiny pasta shape)
2 cups low-sodium chicken broth

In a medium saucepan, melt the butter over medium-high heat. When the butter foams, add the rice and pasta and cook, stirring frequently, until the grains are coated and slightly translucent on the edges. Add the broth and bring to a boil over high heat. Partially cover the saucepan and continue to boil for 10 minutes. Reduce the heat to low. Cover completely and simmer for 15–20 minutes or until most of the liquid has been absorbed.

Makes about 3 cups

FARRO, BARLEY, OR BROWN RICE PILAF

You can find farro at many health food stores and even at larger grocery stores. It has a nutty taste and firm texture and is a wonderfully hearty grain. Barley and brown rice are more widely available than farro and also have a nice bite to their texture.

2 tablespoons butter
2 scallions or ½ small onion, finely chopped
1 cup farro, barley, or brown rice
2 cups low-sodium chicken or beef broth

In a medium saucepan, melt the butter over medium-high heat. When the butter foams, add the scallions or onion and cook, stirring occasionally, for 3 minutes or until tender. Stir in the farro, barley, or rice and cook, stirring frequently, until the grains are coated. Add the broth and bring to a boil over high heat. Partially cover the saucepan and continue to boil for 10 minutes. Reduce the heat to low. Cover completely and simmer for 15–20 minutes or until most of the liquid has been absorbed.

Makes about 3 cups

MEXICAN RICE

1 tablespoon olive oil
½ small onion, finely chopped
1 cup rice
1½ cups low-sodium chicken broth
3 tablespoons tomato paste

In a medium saucepan, heat the oil over medium-high heat. Add the onion and cook, stirring occasionally, for 3 minutes or until translucent. Stir in the rice and cook, stirring frequently, until the grains are coated and slightly translucent on the edges. Stir in the broth and tomato paste until well-blended. Bring to a boil over high heat and continue boiling for 5 minutes. Reduce the heat to low, cover, and simmer for 10 minutes or until the liquid is absorbed and the rice is tender. To serve, fluff with a fork.

Makes about 2 cups

VEGETARIAN BLACK BEANS AND RICE

This dish was inspired by Alexei's friend Daniel, who eats black beans right out of the can like jelly beans—maybe it was his early summers in Sante Fe. Beans are protein packed and a valuable part of any child's diet, vegetarian or otherwise.

1 tablespoon olive oil
½ small onion, finely chopped
1 cup rice
2 cups low-sodium chicken broth
1 cup canned black beans, rinsed and drained
1 small tomato, seeded and finely chopped

In a medium saucepan, heat the oil over medium-high heat. Add the onion and cook, stirring occasionally, for 3 minutes or until translucent. Stir in the rice and cook, stirring frequently, until the grains are coated and slightly translucent on the edges. Stir in the broth and beans. Bring to a boil over high heat and continue boiling for 5 minutes. Stir in the tomato. Reduce the heat to low, cover, and simmer for 10 minutes or until the liquid is absorbed and the rice is tender. To serve, fluff with a fork.

Makes about 2 cups

Peanut Sesame Noodles

This no-cook sauce is a sweet yet savory dish that will appeal to peanut butter lovers. First timers will delight in seeing their favorite peanut butter on noodles. If your child is allergic to peanuts, try the No-Peanut Sesame Noodles on the opposite page.

12 ounces Chinese egg noodles or any straight pasta
½ cup creamy natural peanut butter
¼ cup sesame oil
3 tablespoons low-sodium soy sauce
1 tablespoon maple syrup
½ cup chopped cucumber

Cook the noodles or pasta according to package directions. Drain and reserve about ½ of the cooking water.

While the noodles are cooking, in a large serving bowl, whisk together the peanut butter, oil, soy sauce, and syrup until smooth. If you're using all-natural peanut butter, which tends to be drier than some conventional ones, you may need to add a few tablespoons of the reserved cooking water to loosen the sauce. Add the cooked noodles and toss until evenly coated. Top with the cucumber and serve.

Makes about 3 cups

No-Peanut Sesame Noodles

This nut-free recipe is delicious, even if your child doesn't have a peanut allergy.

12	ounces Chinese egg noodles or any straight pasta
½	cup tahini
5	tablespoons toasted sesame oil
3	tablespoons low-sodium soy sauce
1	teaspoon maple syrup
1	tablespoon sesame seeds
½	cup chopped cucumber

Cook the noodles or pasta according to package directions. Drain and reserve about ½ of the cooking water.

While the noodles are cooking, in a small saucepan, heat the tahini and 2 tablespoons of the oil over low heat, stirring constantly, until smooth. Stir in the remaining 3 tablespoons oil, soy sauce, and syrup. Remove from the heat and stir in the sesame seeds and enough of the reserved cooking water to achieve a "light cream" consistency. In a large serving bowl, toss the sauce with the noodles until evenly coated. Top with the cucumber and serve.

Makes about 3 cups

CRISPY VEGGIE WONTONS

These crispy, veggie-packed wontons are fun to eat. They keep very well in the refrigerator or freezer and heat up in a flash in the toaster oven.

   3 scallions, diced
   2 baby carrots, diced
   1 cup finely shredded cabbage leaves
   1 cup diced shiitake mushrooms
   ½ cup soft tofu
   1 egg, slightly beaten
   2 tablespoons soy sauce
  40 wonton wrappers
   2 tablespoons vegetable oil

In a large bowl, combine the scallions, carrots, cabbage, mushrooms, and tofu, breaking the tofu into small curds. Stir in the egg and soy sauce until the mixture holds together. Fill a small bowl with water.

To assemble the wontons, place 1 teaspoon of the filling in the center of a wonton wrapper. Dip your finger in the water and wet the edges of the wrapper. Bring the edges of the wrapper together, sealing it firmly with your fingers and gently pressing out any air bubbles. This will go much faster than it sounds. Repeat with the remaining wrappers and filling.

In a large skillet, heat 1 tablespoon of the oil over medium-high heat. Add half of the wontons to the pan and cook until the bottoms are browned and crispy, about 2 minutes. Turn the wontons and cook for 2 minutes or until browned and crispy on the other side. Remove to a wire rack to cool. Repeat with the remaining oil and wontons.

Makes 40 wontons

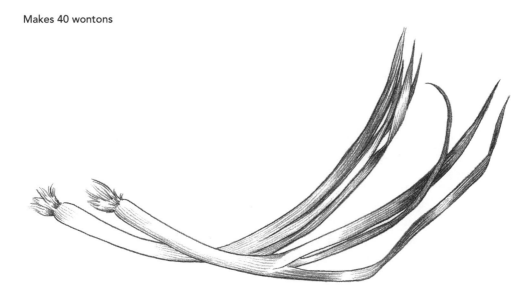

PUMPKIN RAVIOLI

I like the idea of those fresh ravioli at the supermarket, but they often seem filled with such ambiguous ingredients. This mildly seasoned filling makes for an unexpected, though delicious, ravioli that needs no sauce. You can call it pumpkin pie in pasta.

  1   can (14 ounces) pumpkin (not pumpkin pie filling)
  1   tablespoon maple syrup
  1   teaspoon ground cinnamon
  ½   teaspoon mild curry powder
  ½   teaspoon ground ginger
25   wonton wrappers

In a medium bowl, mix together the pumpkin, syrup, cinnamon, curry powder, and ginger until blended. Fill a small bowl with water.

To assemble the ravioli, place 1 teaspoon of the filling in the center of a wonton wrapper. Dip your finger in the water and wet the edges of the wrapper. Bring the edges of the wrapper together, sealing it firmly with your fingers and gently pressing out any air bubbles. This will go much faster than it sounds. Repeat with the remaining wrappers and filling.

In a large saucepan, bring about 3" water to a boil over high heat. In batches, boil no more than 6 ravioli at a time, for 2–3 minutes or until they float to the top, the wrappers are translucent, and the edges tender. Remove with a slotted spoon and serve.

Makes 25 ravioli

BISTRO BITS: These will keep in the fridge for up to 1 week but will not freeze very well. Cooked ravioli only needs 1 minute in boiling water to reheat.

Macaroni and Cheese

The original comfort food. When I first started cooking this dish, I made it with acini de pepe, the "baby" pasta. As Alexei's tastes changed, we've tried pasta alphabets, fusilli, bowties, and other fun shapes.

2 tablespoons butter
2 tablespoons all-purpose flour
1 cup milk
1 cup shredded mild Cheddar cheese
2 cups cooked pasta

In a medium saucepan, melt the butter over medium heat. Reduce the heat to low, add the flour, and cook, stirring constantly, for 2 minutes or until the mixture is bubbly and golden in color. Slowly whisk in the milk. Cook, stirring frequently, for 10 minutes or until the milk thickens. Gradually add the cheese and stir until melted.

Stir in the cooked pasta and serve.

Makes 3 cups

Bistro Bits

• Does your baby love cheese? Try making this recipe with other cheeses like Monterey Jack, Swiss, or goat cheese.

• I usually keep the cheese sauce in a big jar in the refrigerator. Nothing is easier than boiling a little pasta and spooning some sauce over it. I've even been able to get Alexei to eat a little broccoli and zucchini if it has his favorite cheese sauce on top.

BOLOGNESE SAUCE

A favorite family meal in our house, baby at the table or not. This sauce freezes well.

1 pound ground beef
1 medium onion, finely chopped
1 clove garlic, crushed (optional)
2 carrots, finely chopped
1 rib celery, finely chopped
1 can (14 ounces) crushed tomatoes
2 tablespoons tomato paste
  Cooked rice or pasta (optional)

In a large saucepan, brown the ground beef over medium heat, crumbling it with a spoon. Add the onion and garlic (if using) and cook, stirring occasionally, for 10 minutes or until the onion is translucent. Stir in the carrots, celery, tomatoes, and tomato paste. Reduce the heat to low and simmer for at least 30 minutes or until the vegetables are tender.

Serve alone or, if desired, over rice or pasta.

Makes about 4 cups

BISTRO BITS: For a tasty alternative vegetarian recipe, substitute 1 pound of mushrooms for the beef. A mixture of regular white mushrooms, shiitake mushrooms, and portobello mushrooms will result in a silky, almost fatty texture that sometimes seems more indulgent than beef.

Alfredo Sauce with Peas

2 tablespoons butter
2 tablespoons all-purpose flour
1 cup milk
1 cup grated Parmesan cheese
½ cup frozen thawed peas
Cooked pasta, rice, or vegetables

In a medium saucepan, melt the butter over medium heat. Reduce the heat to low, add the flour, and cook, stirring constantly, for 2 minutes or until the mixture is bubbly. Stir in the milk. Cook, stirring frequently, for 10 minutes or until the milk thickens. Gradually add the cheese and stir until melted. Stir in the peas.

Serve over pasta, rice, or vegetables.

Makes about 2 cups

Braised Lamb and Leeks

Many pediatricians recommend lamb as baby's first red meat. Alexei loves the robust flavor of this dish. I serve it over couscous.

½ pound ground lamb
5 baby carrots, diced
1 leek, thinly sliced
1 tablespoon all-purpose flour
¾ cup cold water
Cooked couscous, rice, pasta, or mashed potatoes

In a large nonstick skillet, brown the ground lamb over medium-high heat, crumbling it with a spoon. Reduce the heat to low. Add the carrots and leek and cook, stirring occasionally, for 10 minutes or until the vegetables are soft.

In a small bowl, stir the flour into the cold water until dissolved and then stir the flour mixture into the lamb mixture. Cook, stirring occasionally, for 10 minutes.

Serve as is with couscous, rice, pasta, or mashed potatoes or process to a consistency appropriate for your child.

Makes about 3 cups

BISTRO BITS: This dish freezes well, even with couscous or rice, and can be reheated later in the microwave for quick dinners. Put 3–5 tablespoons of rice, couscous, or pasta in a microwave-safe container and top with ½ cup lamb and leeks. Let the food cool completely before covering with the lid and freezing.

LAMB MEATBALLS

These savory, very tasty lamb meatballs are an excellent finger food.

> 1 pound ground lamb
> 1 small onion, minced
> 1 clove garlic, minced
> ½ cup fresh mint or parsley, minced (optional)
> 2 tablespoons vegetable oil

In a medium bowl, mix the lamb, onion, garlic, and mint or parsley, if using, until thoroughly combined. Shape the mixture into 1" balls; you should get 20 meatballs.

In a large skillet, heat the oil over medium-high heat. In batches, cook the meatballs for 5 minutes, turning occasionally, or until cooked through and no longer pink.

Makes about 20 meatballs

BEEF STEW

1 pound ground beef
1 tablespoon butter
2 tablespoons all-purpose flour
1½ cups low-sodium beef broth
1 small onion, chopped
2 carrots, chopped
1 rib celery, chopped
Cooked rice (optional)

In a large nonstick skillet, cook the ground beef over medium heat, crumbling it with a spoon, until cooked through. Use a slotted spoon to remove the beef to a bowl.

Add the butter to the drippings left in the skillet. When the butter is melted, add the flour and cook, stirring constantly, for 2 minutes or until the mixture is bubbly. Stir in the beef broth, scraping the bottom of the pan, and bring to boil over high heat. Add the onion, carrots, and celery and return the beef to the skillet. Reduce the heat to low, cover, and simmer for 30 minutes or until the vegetables are tender.

Serve as is over rice or puree in a blender or food processor for younger palates.

Makes about 3 cups

SHEPHERD'S PIE

This is actually one of my husband's favorite meals, and Alexei started to eat it right off our plates. The smooth mashed-potato topping was an ideal way to introduce new textures of chopped vegetables and ground beef.

2   potatoes, peeled and cut into 1" pieces
1   pound ground beef or lamb
1   small onion, chopped
1   cup tomato sauce
½   cup milk
1   cup frozen thawed mixed vegetables, such
     as peas, carrots, corn, etc.
½   cup shredded Cheddar cheese

Preheat the oven to 375°F.

Put the potatoes in a medium saucepan with enough water to cover. Bring to a boil over high heat. Reduce the heat to medium-high and continue boiling for 10–15 minutes or until the potatoes are tender when pierced with a fork.

While the potatoes are cooking, in a large skillet, cook the ground beef or lamb over medium-high heat, crumbling it with a spoon. Spoon off and discard any excess fat. Add the onion and cook, stirring occasionally, for 10 minutes or until the onion is translucent. Stir in the tomato sauce and remove from the heat.

Drain the potatoes and return them to the saucepan. Add the milk to the potatoes and mash until smooth. Spoon the meat mixture into a 2-quart casserole dish. Top with the frozen vegetables. Cover with the mashed potatoes and sprinkle the Cheddar cheese on top.

Bake for 30–45 minutes or until heated through and the potatoes are just slightly browned.

Makes 6 cups

BISTRO BITS: This recipe will produce a large number of small servings. I've found that the best way to freeze it is in small freezer-safe storage containers. They reheat conveniently in the microwave. You can also spoon it into ice cube trays.

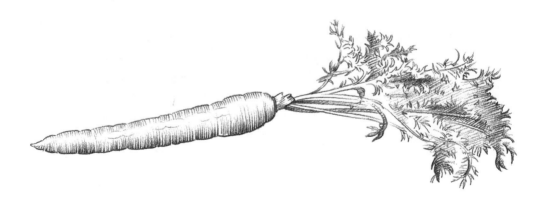

Swedish Meatballs

I've passed this recipe around more often than any other. It's my most reliable dish.

1 pound ground beef
1½ cups milk
½ cup bread crumbs
½ small onion, minced
1 egg
2 tablespoons butter
2 tablespoons all-purpose flour
1 cup low-sodium beef broth
Cooked pasta or rice

In a large bowl, mix the ground beef, ½ cup milk, bread crumbs, onion, and egg until thoroughly combined. Shape into 1" balls. In a large skillet, melt 1 tablespoon of the butter over medium heat. In batches, cook the meatballs, turning occasionally, for 10 minutes or until cooked through and no longer pink. Remove the meatballs from the skillet and set aside. Melt the remaining 1 tablespoon butter in the skillet. Reduce the heat to low, add the flour, and cook, stirring constantly, for 2 minutes or until the mixture is bubbly. Stirring constantly, pour in the broth. Bring to a boil over medium-high heat and continue boiling for 1 minute or until the sauce thickens. Slowly stir in the remaining 1 cup milk. Add the meatballs and stir until evenly coated. Serve over pasta or rice.

Makes about 4 cups

BISTRO BITS: Although you can use a melon baller to make perfect spheres, I find it easiest to scoop up a teaspoonful of meat with one hand and roughly shape it into a ball with the other. Sometimes I end up with Swedish footballs, and Alexei thinks that's a pretty funny thing to call his dinner.

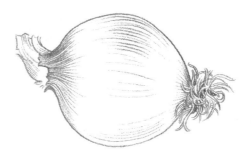

CARNITAS

This very mild version of the traditional Mexican slow-cooked pork is succulent and meltingly tender. A great first introduction to meats.

1–2 pound pork butt or shoulder roast (any fatty cut will do)
1 teaspoon sweet paprika
Hamburger buns (optional)
Barbecue sauce (optional)

Preheat the oven to 275°F.

Put the pork in the center of a 12" piece of aluminum foil. Sprinkle the paprika all over the pork and wrap the foil around the pork. Wrap again in another 12" piece of foil. Place in a roasting pan and bake for at least 4 hours. Resist the temptation to open up the foil to check on the pork for at least 3 hours. The meat should be falling apart and extremely tender. Cool and shred with 2 forks or your fingers.

Serve as is, on hamburger buns with barbecue sauce for older toddlers, or chopped into shorter shreds for younger tots.

Makes about 3 cups

Korean Barbecue

Traditional Korean barbecue is made with well-marbled short ribs. This version is made with ground beef and makes an excellent meal over rice.

1 scallion, minced
1 clove garlic, crushed (optional)
½ cup low-sodium soy sauce
2 tablespoons sugar
1 tablespoon toasted sesame oil
1 pound ground beef
  Cooked rice

In a large bowl, mix the scallion, garlic (if using), soy sauce, sugar, and oil, stirring to dissolve the sugar. Stir in the beef and marinate for at least 15 minutes or even overnight in the refrigerator.

In a large skillet, over medium heat, cook the beef and marinade mixture, crumbling it with a spoon, for 10 minutes or until cooked through and no longer pink. Serve over rice. The juices make a delicious sauce.

Makes about 2 cups

FOIL-STEAMED CHICKEN

My husband, Alex, is very fond of chicken baked in foil, which is really a way of steaming. There's no crispy skin to munch on, but it results in meltingly tender meat with lots of juices to keep it moist. I use the more flavorful leg and thigh portion for Alexei. You can use bone-in breasts— just bake for 10 minutes less.

4 whole chicken legs (thighs attached)

Preheat the oven to 375°F.

Place the chicken in the center of an 18" piece of aluminum foil and wrap completely, sealing any openings. Place the foil package on a baking sheet and bake for 45 minutes. Remove from the oven and let it cool slightly in the foil. Carefully open the foil. The meat should be falling off the bone in a pool of clear juices. Remove the meat from the bones and cut into pieces appropriate for your child.

Makes about 3 cups

CHEDDAR CHICKEN AND BROCCOLI CASSEROLE

I feel very June Cleaver when I make this homey, old-fashioned dinner. Substitute peas, spinach, or any green vegetable for the broccoli.

½ cup rice
1½ cups low-sodium chicken broth
¾ cup finely chopped broccoli florets
¾ cup finely chopped cooked chicken breast (about ½ breast)
½ cup shredded mild Cheddar cheese

In a medium saucepan, bring the rice and broth to a boil over high heat and continue boiling, stirring occasionally, for 5 minutes. Reduce the heat to medium. Cover and simmer for 5 minutes. Stir in the broccoli. Cover and cook for 5 minutes or until the rice is tender but still quite wet. Stir in the chicken and cheese. The cheese will melt into the excess liquid.

Serve as is or puree in a blender or food processor to a consistency appropriate for your child.

Makes about 3 cups

BISTRO BITS: You can freeze this dish in an ice cube tray or small freezer-safe storage containers. The texture of the rice will be slightly gummy upon its defrosting, but it's easily fixed with a pat of butter or a splash of milk.

CURRIED CHICKEN

You may think this dish is too spicy or exotic for your beginner eater, but with its slight sweetness, this mild curry dish is a great way to introduce children to Indian foods.

       1 tablespoon butter
       1 pound ground chicken
       1 small onion, diced
       1 carrot, diced
       1 small zucchini, diced
      ½ cup cold water
       2 tablespoons all-purpose flour
    1–2 tablespoons mild curry powder
       2 tablespoons honey
          Cooked rice (optional)

In a large skillet, melt the butter over medium-high heat and brown the chicken, crumbling it with a spoon. Add the onion, carrot, and zucchini and cook, stirring occasionally, for 10 minutes or until the vegetables are tender.

In a small bowl, whisk together the cold water, flour, and curry powder until blended and stir into the skillet. Bring to a boil over high heat. Reduce the heat to low and cook, stirring occasionally, for 5 minutes or until the curry thickens. Stir in the honey. Serve over rice to older toddlers or puree in a food processor or blender for younger tots.

Makes about 2 cups

CORNMEAL CATFISH

Catfish is a wonderful choice for toddlers. It's a mild, flaky fish that can be completely boneless when properly filleted.

3 tablespoons cornmeal
1 teaspoon sweet paprika
½ teaspoon salt
    Ground black pepper to taste
2 catfish fillets, each cut in half
2 tablespoons vegetable oil

In a shallow bowl, mix the cornmeal, paprika, salt, and pepper. Dredge the catfish fillets in the cornmeal mixture, coating both sides.

In a large skillet, heat the oil over medium-high heat. Add the catfish and cook for 3–5 minutes or until the pieces are golden brown on the bottom. Turn and cook for 3–5 minutes or until cooked through and the fish flakes easily.

Serve either flaked with a fork or cut into small pieces.

Makes about 4 fillets

MARTHA'S VINEYARD COD AND POTATOES

Inspired by our summers spent on Martha's Vineyard, this dish should make use of the freshest, mildest white fish you can find. It is so tender that you can flake it with a fork and stir it into the potatoes. Or, if your baby is ready, you can just feed him small bites right from the fillet.

4 small red bliss potatoes, quartered
½ cup milk
1 small fillet (about ¼ pound) of cod or any mild, white fish
4 crackers (stone-ground wheat, table water, even saltines will do)
1 tablespoon butter

Put the potatoes in a medium saucepan with enough water to cover. Bring to a boil over high heat. Reduce heat to medium-high and continue boiling for 10 minutes or until the potatoes are tender when pierced with a fork. Drain the potatoes and return them to the saucepan. Add the milk and using a potato masher or fork, mash the potatoes until smooth and fluffy.

While the potatoes are cooking, rinse the fish fillet in water and pat dry with a paper towel. Cut into 4 pieces.

Place the crackers in a plastic sandwich bag and crush them into fine crumbs with a rolling pin or the bottom of a heavy glass. Dredge the fish pieces in the cracker crumbs, coating both sides.

In a medium skillet, melt the butter over medium-high heat. Add the fish pieces and cook for 4 minutes or until the pieces are golden brown on the bottom. Turn and cook for 4 minutes or until cooked through and the fish flakes easily. Serve with the mashed potatoes.

Makes 4 fillets and 1 cup potatoes

BISTRO BITS: This dish will freeze best if you flake the fish and stir it into the potatoes. The delicate texture of fish won't stand up to a freezer on its own.

SALMON AND POLENTA

You can hide all sorts of good things in polenta. Even though it's some-thing you usually see on fancy menus, polenta is a simple mixture of cornmeal and water. You can serve it as a "mush," sliced and toasted, or as in this recipe, shaped into patties with delicious add-ins.

4 cups water
1 cup cornmeal
½ cup cooked salmon, or any mild fish
½ cup frozen thawed or fresh corn kernels
2 tablespoons olive oil

Lightly oil a 13" × 9" baking dish.

In a large saucepan, bring the water and cornmeal to a boil over high heat. Continue boiling, stirring frequently, for 15 minutes or until it resembles a mush or cornbread batter. Flake the salmon into small pieces and add to the polenta with the corn. Thoroughly mix and then pour into the baking dish. Cover with plastic wrap and chill for 2 hours or until set.

Cut the polenta into approximately 2½" × 1½" triangles or squares, or use a cookie cutter for fun shapes. In a large skillet, heat 1 tablespoon oil over medium-high heat and cook the polenta pieces for 2 minutes on each side or until lightly browned and crispy. Repeat with the remaining polenta pieces and oil.

Makes about 16 pieces

BISTRO BITS: For beginning eaters, skip the chilling altogether and serve as a soft polenta after stirring in the salmon and corn. Cool slightly and serve with a spoon.

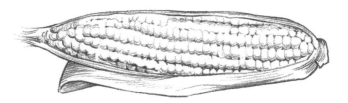

CHAPTER 7

SNACKS AND BEVERAGES

The eternal quest for healthy snacks your child will actually eat is often compromised into graham crackers and a juice box. Very few children will eat the prescribed three meals a day with two light snacks in between. Most toddlers I know are very unpredictable about their meals, so their snack times take on greater importance than most parents would like. Many pediatricians would say that this is not such a bad thing in that small meals are generally more easily digested than larger meals and as long as snacks are healthy, there's no reason to discourage nutritious eating, even if it is outside of the regular mealtimes.

So how do we compete with cleverly packaged cookies and chips or fun, shiny juice boxes? Make your homemade snacks as tasty as any store-bought version and try to offer a variety of foods. Many of these snack recipes will keep for days if not weeks; offer something different every day.

Every week I try to make a pitcher of a delicious, low-sugar beverage like Kiwi-Lime Aqua Fresca (page 172) or Watermelon Punch (page 170), and Alexei is fascinated by their bright colors, yummy flavors, and sheer novelty. All this being said with good intentions, don't let the snack aisle become a forbidden land to further pique your child's curiosity. I admit to keeping a small plastic storage bag of "bribes" in my diaper bag, just for emergencies and travel. These commercially made cookies or candies come out on rare occasion, and therefore haven't lost their wow factor (yet). In the meantime, the entire family has turned into a bunch of very healthy snackers.

In this chapter...

GRANOLA

It's not for hippies anymore. Some store-bought granola can be very high in sugar and fat, so this homemade version is well worth the small amount of effort.

2 cups quick-cooking oats
Up to 2 cups in total of sesame seeds, unsweetened flaked coconut, sunflower seeds, chopped or slivered nuts (almonds, peanuts, walnuts, pecans, and pine nuts), and/or puffed rice cereal
½ cup maple syrup
2 tablespoons vegetable oil

Preheat the oven to 300°F. Line a baking sheet with aluminum foil.

In a large bowl, stir together the oats, seeds, coconut, nuts, and/or cereal. Add the maple syrup and oil and toss to coat well. Spread evenly on the prepared baking sheet, no thicker than ½". Bake, stirring once halfway through, for 25 minutes. Remove from the oven and let cool completely. Break into pieces.

Makes about 5–6 cups

BISTRO BITS

• I keep bags of homemade granola in the cupboard for up to 2 weeks. Or it will keep in the fridge for longer. It's a great snack and a healthy, crunchy topping.

• Break granola into larger pieces or bars for easy, on-the-go snacks.

• Put the granola in a sturdy plastic storage or freezer bag and crush with a meat mallet or rolling pin and use as a topping for yogurt, fresh fruit, and ice cream.

CHEWY CRANBERRY-OATMEAL COOKIES

½ cup all-purpose flour
½ teaspoon salt
½ cup butter, melted
½ cup packed brown sugar
1 egg
1½ cups quick-cooking oats
¾ cup chopped cranberries

Preheat the oven to 350°F.

In a small bowl, combine the flour and salt. In a large bowl, with an electric mixer on medium-high speed, cream the butter and brown sugar. Add the egg and beat until blended.

Gradually beat in the flour mixture until blended. Stir in the oats and cranberries.

Drop by teaspoonfuls onto an ungreased baking sheet, at least 2" apart. Bake for 12–15 minutes or until golden. Remove from the oven and cool on a rack for 1 minute. Remove the cookies to the rack and cool completely.

Makes about 3 dozen

OATMEAL–CHOCOLATE CHIP COOKIES

1½ cups all-purpose flour
1 teaspoon baking powder
½ teaspoon baking soda
½ teaspoon salt
½ cup butter, softened
½ cup packed brown sugar
1 egg
2 teaspoons vanilla extract
1 cup quick-cooking oats
½ cup mini chocolate chips

Preheat the oven to 350°F.

In a medium bowl, combine the flour, baking powder, baking soda, and salt until blended. In a large bowl, with an electric mixer on medium-high speed, cream the butter, brown sugar, egg, and vanilla until blended. Gradually beat in the flour mixture until blended. Stir in the oats and chocolate chips.

Drop by teaspoonfuls onto an ungreased baking sheet, at least 2" apart. Bake for 10–12 minutes or until golden. Remove from the oven and cool on a rack for 1 minute. Remove the cookies to the rack and cool completely.

Makes about 4 dozen

MARMALADE COOKIES

These are simple butter cookies that are sweetened with marmalade instead of sugar. Use any fruit juice–sweetened jam, jelly, or preserve.

1½ cups all-purpose flour
2 teaspoons baking powder
½ teaspoon salt
½ cup butter, softened
¾ cup your favorite fruit juice–sweetened marmalade, jelly, or jam
1 egg
1 teaspoon vanilla extract

Preheat the oven to 350°F. Line a baking sheet with parchment paper.

In a medium bowl, combine the flour, baking powder, and salt until blended.

In a large bowl, with an electric mixer on medium-high speed, beat the butter; marmalade, jelly, or jam; egg; and vanilla until blended. Gradually beat in the flour mixture until blended. The dough will be streaked with marmalade.

Drop by teaspoonfuls onto the prepared baking sheet, at least 2" apart. Bake for 12 minutes or until golden. Remove from the oven and cool on a rack for 1 minute. Remove the cookies to the rack and cool completely.

Makes about 3 dozen

Secret Fruit Bars

A "secret" fruit bar sure sounds a lot more appetizing than a "carrot and fruit" bar, doesn't it? Kids love these fruity bars, and parents love sneaking in some veggies.

   2 apples, cored and chopped
1½ cups shredded carrots
   1 cup dried cranberries
   1 cup fresh or frozen thawed blueberries, cranberries, or strawberries
   ½ cup water
   4 cups quick-cooking oats
   2 cups all-purpose flour
   1 cup packed brown sugar
   1 teaspoon baking soda
   1 teaspoon ground cinnamon
   ½ teaspoon salt
   1 cup butter, cut into small pieces

Preheat the oven to 350°F. Line a 13" × 9" baking pan with parchment paper.

In a medium saucepan, bring the apples; carrots; dried cranberries; blueberries, cranberries, or strawberries; and water to a boil over high heat. Reduce the heat to low and simmer, stirring occasionally, for 15 minutes or until the apples are soft and juices are syrupy. Remove from the heat and cool.

In a large bowl, combine the oats, flour, brown sugar, baking soda, cinnamon, and salt until blended. Using a pastry blender or 2 knives, cut in the butter until the mixture makes coarse crumbs.

Evenly press ½ of the oat mixture into the prepared baking pan. Evenly spread the fruit mixture on top. Top with the remaining oat mixture, pressing gently with the palm of your hand to even out the top.

Bake for 35–45 minutes or until golden. Cool completely on a wire rack. To serve, cut into 1½" × 2" bars.

Makes about 3 dozen

Peanut Butter and Jam Cookies

I like the idea of making everyday foods sound special. These yummy cookies put a different spin on the old PB&J.

1½ cups all-purpose flour
1 teaspoon baking powder
½ teaspoon baking soda
½ cup creamy natural peanut butter
¼ cup butter, softened
¼ cup packed brown sugar
1 egg
1 teaspoon vanilla extract
½ cup your favorite fruit juice–sweetened jam or jelly

Preheat the oven to 350°F. Line a baking sheet with parchment paper; set aside.

In a medium bowl, combine the flour, baking powder, and baking soda until blended.

In a large bowl, using a rubber spatula, stir together the peanut butter and butter until blended. Stir in the brown sugar, egg, and vanilla until smooth. Stir in the flour mixture until blended.

Using your hands, shape the dough into 1-tablespoon balls and place them on the prepared baking sheet, at least 2" apart. With your thumb, gently press into the center of each ball, creating an indentation for the jam or jelly. Spoon ¼–½ teaspoon of jam or jelly into the center of each cookie. Bake for 12 minutes or until golden. Remove from the oven and cool on a rack for 1 minute. Remove the cookies to the rack and cool completely.

Makes about 3 dozen

Egg-Free Shortbread Cookies

Poor little tykes who are allergic to eggs often miss out on treats. This is a classic shortbread recipe that can be used for any shape of cookie. These make great holiday cookies. Try topping with colored icings or sprinkles for Halloween, Christmas, or birthdays.

> 1½ cups all-purpose flour
> ¼ cup sugar
> ¼ cup butter, cut into small pieces

Preheat the oven to 325°F.

In a large bowl, combine the flour and sugar until blended. Using a pastry blender or 2 knives, cut in the butter until the mixture resembles coarse crumbs.

Using your hands, shape the dough into a ball and knead on a lightly floured surface until it is smooth. Using a floured rolling pin, roll the dough out to about ½" thickness. Using assorted cookie cutters, cut out into desired shapes and place the cookies on an ungreased baking sheet. Bake for 20 minutes or until golden. Remove from the oven and cool on a rack for 1 minute. Remove the cookies to the rack and cool completely.

Makes about 2 dozen

Bistro Bits: For chocolate shortbread, add ½ cup cocoa to the flour mixture.

BANANA BARS

The key to these sweet, though low-sugar, bar cookies is an abundance of ripe bananas, beat until almost pureed.

2½ cups all-purpose flour
2 teaspoons baking powder
½ teaspoon salt
3 very ripe bananas
½ cup butter, softened
½ cup packed brown sugar
1 egg
1 teaspoon vanilla extract

Preheat the oven to 350°F. Grease a 9" × 9" square baking pan.

In a large bowl, combine the flour, baking powder, and salt until blended.

In a large bowl, with an electric mixer on medium speed, beat the bananas until they are nearly pureed. Beat in the butter, brown sugar, egg, and vanilla until smooth. Gradually beat in the flour mixture until blended. The batter will be rather stiff.

Evenly spread the batter into the prepared baking pan. Bake for 20 minutes or until golden. Cool completely on a wire rack. To serve, cut into 1½" squares.

Makes about 3 dozen

Gingersnaps

A handful of chopped raisins helps keep these cookies moist.

    2 cups all-purpose flour
 1½ teaspoons ground cinnamon
    1 teaspoon baking soda
    1 teaspoon ground ginger
  ½ cup butter, softened
  ½ cup packed brown sugar
  ½ cup dark molasses
    1 egg
  ½ cup chopped raisins

Preheat the oven to 350°F.

In a large bowl, combine the flour, cinnamon, baking soda, and ginger.

In a large bowl, with an electric mixer on medium speed, beat the butter, brown sugar, molasses, and egg until blended. Gradually beat in the flour mixture until blended. Stir in the raisins.

Using your hands, shape the dough into 1" balls and place them on an ungreased baking sheet, at least 2" apart.

Bake for 8–10 minutes or until edges look set and the tops begin to crack. Remove from the oven and cool on a rack for 1 minute. Remove the cookies to the rack and cool completely.

Makes about 3 dozen

Coconut Macaroons

These will not be as dense as store-bought macaroons, but they still have a rich coconut flavor.

2 egg whites
2 cups unsweetened flaked coconut
¼ cup unsweetened condensed milk
1 teaspoon vanilla extract
½–¾ cup powdered sugar

Preheat the oven to 350°F. Line a baking sheet with parchment paper.

In a large bowl, with an electric mixer on high speed, beat the egg whites until they can hold a stiff peak. Gently fold in the coconut, condensed milk, vanilla, and ½ cup of the powdered sugar. If the mixture is too loose to form balls, fold in the remaining ¼ cup powdered sugar. Do not worry about liquid that pools at the bottom of the bowl.

Drop by generous tablespoonfuls onto the prepared baking sheet. Bake for 20 minutes, or until the tops and edges are lightly browned. Remove from the oven and cool on a rack for 1 minute. Remove the cookies to the rack and cool completely.

Makes about 2 dozen

Peanut Butter Balls

My friend Leslie inspired this recipe. She remembered her health-conscious mom serving a similar treat to neighborhood kids when she was growing up.

1 cup granola (use a good-quality store-
bought or make your own on page 142)
1 cup creamy natural peanut butter
½ cup chopped raisins
¼ cup honey

Put the granola in a heavy plastic storage bag and crush it into smaller pieces with a meat mallet or rolling pin.

In a medium bowl, combine the peanut butter, raisins, honey, and ½ of the crushed granola and stir until blended. Using your hands or a melon baller, shape the peanut butter mixture into 1" balls. Roll each ball in the remaining ½ cup crushed granola.

Place on a baking sheet and chill until set, about 1 hour.

Makes about 20 balls

CINNAMON CRISPS

2 flour tortillas (about 10" each)
2 tablespoons water
1 tablespoon butter, melted
1 teaspoon ground cinnamon
1 teaspoon sugar

Preheat the oven to 350°F. Line a baking sheet with parchment paper.

Cut the tortillas into wedges or use a cookie cutter for fun shapes.

In a small bowl, combine the water and butter and stir briskly with a fork. In another small bowl, combine the cinnamon and sugar until blended. Lay the tortilla pieces on the prepared baking sheet. Brush with the butter mixture and then sprinkle with the cinnamon mixture.

Bake for 10 minutes or until golden and crisp.

Makes about 15 crisps

Sourdough Crisps

While I was writing this book, the dangers of trans fat came screaming into the news. The experts agree that no amount is safe in our diets, but trans fat seems as ubiquitous as salt. Slowly but surely we've been trying to cut back on trans fats and began with all those store-bought crackers in the cupboard. These crispy flats are positively addictive, and keep for up to 2 weeks in an airtight container.

1   small round loaf sourdough bread
3   tablespoons olive oil
    Coarse sea salt
    Sweet paprika, sweet curry powder, or
    cayenne pepper

Preheat the oven to 400°F. Line a baking sheet with parchment paper.

Using a serrated bread knife, slice the sourdough loaf into ¼"-thick slices, as thin as you are able to manage without shredding the bread. Lay the bread slices on the prepared baking sheet. Brush lightly with the oil and then sprinkle with just a pinch of salt and paprika, curry powder, or cayenne pepper. Turn the bread slices over and repeat.

Bake for 10 minutes. The bread will just begin to brown. Flip the crisps over and bake 5 minutes longer. Remove and cool completely. Store in an airtight container.

Makes about 20 crisps

CHEDDAR COINS

An old standby for wine and cheese get-togethers, these Cheddar coins are also one of Alexei's favorite snacks. The dough is simply made and can be kept in the refrigerator in logs to slice up when you want a freshly made snack.

1 cup all-purpose flour
½ cup butter, softened
1 cup shredded Cheddar cheese
¼–½ teaspoon sweet paprika

In a large bowl, with an electric mixer on medium speed, beat the flour and butter until blended. Beat in the cheese and paprika just until blended. On a piece of plastic wrap, form the dough into a log. Wrap and chill for at least 30 minutes.

Preheat the oven to 350°F. Line a baking sheet with parchment paper. Remove the dough from the refrigerator and slice into ⅛"-thick "coins." Place the coins on the baking sheet and bake for 10–12 minutes or until just slightly golden. Remove from the oven and cool on a rack for 1 minute. Remove the coins to the rack and cool completely.

Makes about 3 dozen

Hummus

The hummus you buy at the store can be very high in fat and sodium, and you'd be surprised how much better it tastes when you make it fresh. You can omit the tahini if your child is allergic to sesame.

1 can (14 ounces) chickpeas, rinsed and drained
¼ cup tahini (or substitute ½ teaspoon sea salt)
1 small clove garlic (optional)
Juice of 1 lemon
2 tablespoons olive oil

In a blender or food processor, puree the chickpeas, tahini, garlic (if using), lemon juice, and oil until smooth.

Makes about 2 cups

BISTRO BITS: Serve as a dip with pita bread wedges or crudités, or serve on pitas for quick, high-protein sandwiches.

Baby Ghanouj

Alex and I spent part of our honeymoon cruising the Turkish coast, and the captain of our boat made the most delicious aubergine salad. It was delectable with its garlic and sweet eggplant. This "baby ghanouj" uses roasted garlic for a much mellower flavor.

5–6 Japanese eggplants
3 large cloves garlic, unpeeled
2 tablespoons olive oil
Juice of 1 lemon
Salt to taste
Pita triangles or crackers

Preheat the oven to 400°F.

Remove the stems from the eggplants. Rub the eggplants and garlic with the olive oil. Place the eggplants and garlic on a baking sheet and roast for 30 minutes or until tender. Let cool slightly.

Carefully peel and discard the skin from the eggplants and the garlic, which should come apart very easily from the clove.

In a blender or food processor, puree the eggplant, garlic, lemon juice, and salt until smooth.

Serve on pita triangles or crackers.

Makes about 1½ cups

BISTRO BITS: You may use 1 large Italian eggplant instead of the Japanese ones if desired. Be sure to cut it in half lengthwise before rubbing with the oil. Cook as above.

GUACAMOLE

Many first eaters love the silky texture and mild flavor of avocados. This guacamole is also wonderful as a sandwich spread in place of mayonnaise.

2   very ripe avocados
½   small tomato, seeded and diced
½   very small onion, diced
1   small jalapeño (optional)
     Juice of ½ lemon
½   teaspoon salt
     Crackers, tortilla chips, or crudités

Slice each avocado in half and twist to separate. The pit will remain in 1 half and you can easily remove it by carefully sticking the tip of a sharp knife into it and twisting it out of the flesh.

Scoop the flesh out of the peel and place it in a medium bowl. Add the tomato, onion, jalapeño (if using; wear plastic gloves when handling), lemon juice, and salt and mash with a fork until smooth. I like guacamole a little chunky, but you can puree it to as smooth a consistency as your child likes. Serve with crackers, tortilla chips, or crudités.

Makes about 1 cup

DEVILED EGGS

These delectable reminders of your childhood can be easily stored in the refrigerator for up to 3 days. A very neat way to pack them is to "re-join" 2 halves, yolks facing inward, and wrap tightly in plastic wrap.

> 3 eggs
> 1 tablespoon mayonnaise
> 1 teaspoon chopped chives or minced onion (optional)
> Sweet paprika

Put the eggs in a small saucepan with enough water to cover by 1". Bring to a boil over high heat. Reduce the heat to low and simmer for 10 minutes. Immediately remove the eggs to a colander and rinse with cold water until cool.

Peel the eggs, then slice each in half and remove the yolks to a small bowl. Set the whites aside on a paper towel–lined plate. Add the mayonnaise and chives or onion, if using, to the yolks and mix with a fork until smooth and creamy. Spoon a scant tablespoon of the yolk mixture into each egg white. Sprinkle with paprika.

Makes 6 halves

APPLE SMOOTHIE

This takes the notion of fresh applesauce to a more liquid version.

1   apple, cored and chopped but not peeled
1   cup water
½   teaspoon ground cinnamon
2   ice cubes

In a blender, puree the apple, water, cinnamon, and ice cubes until smooth.

Makes about 2 cups

ORANGEADE

Nothing tastes better than freshly squeezed orange juice. My husband is particularly fond of squeezing oranges on a lazy Sunday morning. Fresh orange juice tends to be sweeter than commercial juice and has less acidity.

2   juicing oranges
1   cup water

Cut the oranges in half and using a citrus reamer or juicer, extract as much juice as possible. Depending on the size of your oranges, you'll get up to ½ cup. In a large measuring cup, combine the orange juice and water.

Makes about 1½ cups

BANANA MILK

I used to drink this back in my single days when I had a craving for a milk shake. It's a sweet, cool alternative to more fortified smoothies and shakes.

1 small ripe banana
1 cup milk
1 tablespoon honey
   Dash of ground cinnamon
2 ice cubes

In a blender, puree the banana, milk, honey, cinnamon, and ice cubes until smooth.

Makes about 2 cups

LEMONADE

Lemonade is usually very high in sugar, so this recipe adds in some fresh orange juice for sweetness. Store-bought orange juice will not be as sweet.

6 cups water
½ cup sugar
4 lemons
2 juicing oranges

In a 2-cup microwave-safe measuring cup, combine 1 cup water and the sugar. Microwave on high for 10–15 seconds. Carefully stir to dissolve the sugar.

Using a citrus reamer or juicer, extract as much juice as possible from the lemons and oranges. Strain the seeds and pour the juice into a 2-quart pitcher. Stir in the sugar syrup and remaining 5 cups water. Chill until ready to serve.

Makes about 7 cups

Horchata

I've had every version of this possible. Sometimes it's light and refreshing and at other times thick and rich like a milk shake. This version will be thinner, with a clear cinnamon flavor, and is a great substitute for milk.

4 cups water
1 cup rice
½ cup sugar
2 cinnamon sticks

In a large bowl, combine all of the ingredients and let sit for about 3 hours.

Pour the rice mixture into a large saucepan. Bring to a boil over high heat and continue boiling for 10 minutes. Reduce the heat to low and simmer for 30 minutes. Let the rice mixture cool slightly in the pot. Remove and discard the cinnamon sticks.

In batches, puree the rice mixture in a blender or food processor until smooth and creamy.

Makes about 6 cups

BABY BELLINIS

It seems a shame to leave our children out of special champagne-worthy occasions. A baby Bellini in a fun, plastic champagne flute makes them feel very special indeed.

1   very ripe white peach (a yellow peach is fine)
2   cups seltzer water

Peel and pit the peach, then slice into quarters.

In a blender, puree the peach and seltzer water until smooth.

Makes about 2½ cups

BERRY SMOOTHIE

1   cup fresh or frozen thawed berries (any kind will do)
½   cup plain yogurt
½   cup milk
2   ice cubes

In a blender, puree the berries, yogurt, milk, and ice cubes until smooth.

Makes about 2 cups

CHOCOLATE-BANANA SMOOTHIE

1 small ripe banana
½ cup plain yogurt
½ cup milk
2 tablespoons chocolate syrup
2 ice cubes

In a blender, puree the banana, yogurt, milk, chocolate syrup, and ice cubes until smooth.

Makes about 1½ cups

PEACH MELBA SMOOTHIE

1 cup sliced fresh or frozen peaches
½ cup fresh or frozen thawed raspberries
½ cup plain yogurt
½ cup orange juice
2 ice cubes

In a blender, puree the peaches, raspberries, yogurt, orange juice, and ice cubes until smooth.

Makes about 2 cups

ORANGE-PEACH SMOOTHIE

1 cup sliced fresh or frozen peaches
1 orange, peeled and seeds removed
½ cup plain yogurt
½ cup orange juice
2 ice cubes

In a blender, puree the peaches, orange, yogurt, orange juice, and ice cubes until smooth.

Makes about 2½ cups

MANGO LAHSSI

One of the most delicious desserts I've ever had was a tall, chilled glass of this mango beverage at an Indian restaurant. It's really just a simple mango smoothie.

1 very ripe mango, peeled, seeded, and chopped
1 cup milk
1 cup plain yogurt

In a blender, puree the mango, milk, and yogurt until smooth.

Makes about 3 cups

PINEAPPLE-BANANA SMOOTHIE

Sweet banana and refreshing pineapple make for a delicious baby piña colada that's also a source of vitamin C.

1 small ripe banana
½ cup fresh pineapple chunks
½ cup plain yogurt
½ cup milk

In a blender, combine the banana, pineapple, yogurt, and milk and pulse a few times. Puree on high speed for 1 minute.

Makes about 2 cups

BISTRO BITS: You can add water to this smoothie to thin out the consistency and give it to your child in a sippy cup with the nonspill valve removed.

WATERMELON PUNCH

That huge watermelon always looks like such a good idea at the market, doesn't it? Now you have a use for the leftovers. This is the easiest, and prettiest, punch.

1 cup watermelon chunks, seeds removed
½ cup white grape juice

In a blender, puree the watermelon and grape juice until smooth. Serve in sippy cups or with a straw.

Makes about 1½ cups

BISTRO BITS

- On a hot day, or when your child is teething, using partially frozen watermelon makes for refreshing slushies to eat with a spoon.
- Since watermelons are large, you can easily double or triple this recipe!

WATERMELON AQUA FRESCA

1½ cups water
   ¼ cup sugar
    2 cups watermelon chunks, seeds removed
       Juice of 1 lime

In a 2-cup microwave-safe measuring cup, combine ½ cup of the water and the sugar. Microwave on high power for 5–10 seconds. Carefully stir to dissolve the sugar and form a syrup.

In a 1½-quart pitcher, mash the watermelon with a wooden spoon until the flesh breaks down and becomes pulpy and juicy. Stir in the sugar syrup, the remaining 1 cup water, and the lime juice. Chill until ready to serve.

Makes about 3½ cups

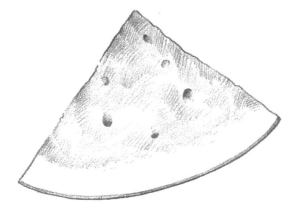

KIWI-LIME AQUA FRESCA

Your little ones will delight in this brilliant green cooler.

2   very ripe kiwis, peeled and quartered
2   cups water
    Juice of 1 lime

In a blender, puree the kiwis, 1 cup of water, and the lime juice until smooth. Stir in the remaining 1 cup water. Chill until ready to serve.

Makes about 2½ cups

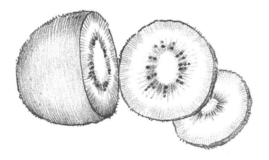

STRAWBERRY PUNCH

Weaning Alexei from the bottle was 3 straight weeks of begging, crying, and frustration—and that was just me! It did, however, result in some very yummy beverage recipes that I thought would make his sippy cup more tempting.

1½ cups water
½ cup fresh strawberries, hulled and cleaned

In a blender, puree the water and strawberries until smooth.

Makes about 1½ cups

BISTRO BITS

- You can serve this in a sippy cup, though you may need to take the nonspill valve out.
- This is a wonderful alternative to apple juice, which many pediatricians suggest babies drink too much of.
- Strawberries work the best of any berries for this recipe. Blueberries have a skin and raspberries have larger seeds.

CHAPTER 8

SPECIAL OCCASIONS AND TREATS

This was the most challenging chapter for me to write. I've never been a great baker. My breads always had a raw core, cakes were lopsided, and many cookies could have been used as hockey pucks. The precision and accuracy required for truly impressive desserts has always been beyond my patience. I also have a tragic sweet tooth (ask my dentist), so store-bought treats always tasted better to me. This all changed with Alexei's increasing interest in sweets, cakes, cookies—you name it—just like any other toddler. I was very concerned about not only his nutrition, but also his teeth! I found that homemade desserts and treats called for far less sugar than I'd imagined and that commercially made sweets contained far more additives to maintain their toothsome texture than I'd ever realized. This is truly a part of your child's diet that you can vastly improve by making yourself.

Nevertheless, even if you make every crumb of cake your child ever eats, the guiding principle of sweets is moderation. In preparation, use less sugar when possible, as in cake batters, and in serving treats to your child, keep the scarcity value as high as possible. If you're constantly using food as a bribe or reward, it won't seem as special. That being said, some treats can be very healthy, and I happily indulge Alexei quite often before he is too old to realize how well he is eating.

In this chapter...

LIGHT CHOCOLATE CAKE

This easy cake is light on sugar and also admittedly light on chocolate. It contains just enough of both to make it a treat.

1¼ cups all-purpose flour
1 teaspoon baking powder
½ teaspoon baking soda
Dash of salt
⅓ cup semisweet chocolate chips
3 tablespoons butter
1 egg
½ cup packed brown sugar
½ cup milk
1 teaspoon vanilla extract
Frosting of your choice (pages 185–188)

Preheat the oven to 350°F. Grease a 9" × 9" baking pan.

In a large bowl, whisk together the flour, baking powder, baking soda, and salt.

In a small microwave-safe bowl or measuring cup, combine the chocolate chips and butter. Microwave on high for 10–30 seconds. Stir until the chocolate is melted; let cool.

In a large bowl, with an electric mixer on medium speed, beat the egg, brown sugar, milk, and vanilla until blended. Beat in the cooled chocolate mixture until blended. Gradually beat in the flour mixture until blended.

Pour into the prepared pan. Bake for 20 minutes or until a toothpick inserted in the center comes out clean. Remove from the oven and cool on a rack for 10 minutes. Remove the cake to the rack and cool completely. Frost and cut into 16 squares.

Makes 16 squares

BISTRO BITS: To make Light Chocolate Cupcakes, grease a 12-cup muffin pan or simply line with cupcake liners. Prepare Light Chocolate Cake batter as directed. Fill each muffin cup about ⅔ full. Bake for 15 minutes or until a toothpick inserted in the center comes out clean. Remove from the oven and let cool completely on a wire rack.

GIFT BAGS

I know many parents stress out about the look and quality of the goody bags given to guests at the end of the party, but just think of it as what it is intended to be: a nice thank-you for coming. Some simple treats to put in any gift bag or just tie with a ribbon are:

Soap bubbles

Bars of fun soap

A short stack of cookies wrapped in paper

Small bath toys

Travel-size sunscreen and sunglasses

Inexpensive photo magnets or albums

Vanilla Cupcakes

I found it a better compromise to use sugar more generously in frostings and cut back significantly for the cake recipes. After all, the frosting is the best part. This cake recipe calls for just ½ cup of brown sugar, though has a pleasantly mild vanilla flavor.

    1 cup all-purpose flour
    ½ cup packed brown sugar
    2 teaspoons baking powder
    1 teaspoon salt
    ¼ cup butter, softened
    1 egg
    1 cup buttermilk or plain yogurt
    1 teaspoon vanilla extract
      Frosting of your choice (pages 185–188)

Preheat the oven to 375°F. Grease a 12-cup muffin pan or simply line with cupcake liners.

In a large bowl, whisk together the flour, brown sugar, baking powder, and salt.

In a large bowl, with an electric mixer on medium speed, beat the butter, egg, buttermilk or yogurt, and vanilla until blended. Gradually beat in the flour mixture until blended. Fill each muffin cup about ⅔ full.

Bake for 19 minutes or until a toothpick inserted in the center comes out clean.

Remove from the oven and cool on a rack for 3 minutes. Remove the cupcakes to the rack and cool completely.

Makes 12 cupcakes

PEANUT BUTTER CAKE

I frost this with Vanilla Cream Cheese Frosting (page 186).

> 2 cups all-purpose flour
> ½ cup packed brown sugar
> 2 teaspoons baking powder
> 1 teaspoon baking soda
> Dash of salt
> 1 cup milk
> 2 eggs
> 2 tablespoons creamy natural peanut butter, softened
> Frosting of your choice (pages 185–188)

Preheat the oven to 350°F. Grease a 9" × 9" baking pan.

In a large bowl, whisk together the flour, brown sugar, baking powder, baking soda, and salt. With an electric mixer on medium speed, beat the milk, eggs, and peanut butter until blended. Gradually beat in the flour mixture. Pour into the prepared baking pan.

Bake for 25–30 minutes or until a toothpick inserted in the center comes out clean. Remove from the oven and cool on a rack for 10 minutes. Remove the cake to the rack and cool completely. Frost and cut into 16 squares.

Makes 16 squares

BISTRO BITS: To make Peanut Butter Cupcakes, grease a 12-cup muffin pan or simply line with cupcake liners. Prepare Peanut Butter Cake batter as directed. Fill each muffin cup about ⅔ full. Bake for 15 minutes or until a toothpick inserted in the center comes out clean. Remove from the oven and let cool completely on a wire rack.

CARROT CAKE

This is especially good topped with Vanilla Cream Cheese Frosting (page 186).

1 cup all-purpose flour
½ cup packed brown sugar
2 teaspoons baking soda
1 teaspoon baking powder
1 teaspoon ground cinnamon
½ cup butter
2 eggs
2 cups shredded carrots
   Vanilla Cream Cheese Frosting (page 186)

Preheat the oven to 350°F. Grease a 9" × 9" baking pan.

In a large bowl, whisk together the flour, brown sugar, baking soda, baking powder, and cinnamon. In a large bowl, with an electric mixer, beat the butter and eggs until blended. Stir in the carrots and the flour mixture until blended. Pour into the prepared baking pan. Bake for 30 minutes or until a toothpick inserted in the center comes out clean. Remove from the oven and cool on a rack for 10 minutes. Remove the cake to the rack and cool completely. Frost and cut into 16 squares.

Makes 16 squares

GINGERBREAD

As a child I often mistook dark, spicy gingerbread for chocolate cake. It was a disappointment only until I found gingerbread to be just as delicious, especially with a dollop of freshly whipped cream.

1½ cups all-purpose flour
1 teaspoon baking powder
1 teaspoon ground cinnamon
½ teaspoon baking soda
½ teaspoon ground ginger
½ cup butter
½ cup dark molasses
1 egg
Confectioners' sugar or whipped cream (optional)

Preheat the oven to 350°F. Grease a 9" × 9" baking pan.

In a large bowl, whisk together the flour, baking powder, cinnamon, baking soda, and ginger.

In a large bowl, with an electric mixer, beat together the butter, molasses, and egg until blended. Gradually beat in the flour mixture until blended. Pour into the prepared pan. Bake for 25–35 minutes or until a toothpick inserted in the center comes out clean. Remove from the oven and cool on a rack for 10 minutes. Remove the cake to the rack and cool completely. Cut into 16 squares.

Serve this plain, with a dusting of confectioners' sugar, or with a spoonful of whipped cream.

Makes 16 squares

STRAWBERRY SHORTCAKE

At the height of summer, it's hard not to eat the strawberries on the way home from the market. The ripest, sweetest berries require almost no sugar at all to bring out their naturally toothsome syrup. Because the strawberries provide so much flavor, I don't even sweeten the biscuits.

1 pint ripe strawberries, hulled and sliced
1 tablespoon confectioners' sugar
Squeeze of fresh lemon
2 cups all-purpose flour
1½ teaspoons baking powder
½ teaspoon salt
¼ cup butter
½ cup milk
Freshly whipped cream (optional)

Preheat the oven to 350°F.

In a medium bowl or plastic storage container, toss the strawberries, confectioners' sugar, and lemon juice until evenly coated. Cover and let sit for at least 30 minutes, or up to overnight in the refrigerator.

In a large bowl, combine the flour, baking powder, and salt until blended. Using a pastry blender or 2 knives, cut in the butter until the mixture has a coarse, mealy texture. Stir in the milk until a ball of dough forms.

On a lightly floured surface, knead the dough for just 30 seconds, or about 8 turns. Using a floured rolling pin, roll the dough out to about ½" thickness. Using a 2"–3" biscuit or cookie cutter or the rim of a glass, cut into the desired shapes. Gently place the biscuits on an ungreased baking sheet, at least 1" apart. Bake for 10–12 minutes or until golden brown. Remove from the oven and cool on a rack for 15 minutes.

To assemble, place 1 biscuit and ½ cup strawberry topping on each plate. Top, if desired, with a dollop of freshly whipped cream.

Makes 12 shortcakes

CAKE IDEAS

For Alexei's first birthday I drew up some fairly elaborate sketches for a birthday cake to resemble a small tower of building blocks, with very particular instructions about colors and exactly which letters to put on the blocks. The bakery staff was probably wondering what kind of nervous child this neurotic woman was raising. The cake turned out to be beautifully constructed, though in the excitement and chaos of Alexei's birthday party (held in a bright, sunny park) its elaborate architecture melted in the hot September sun. It was still delicious, and the kids had fun poking at the piles of icing. Lesson learned: I'll save the cake anxiety for his wedding and just bake some simple cupcakes in the meantime.

Banana Cake

1 cup all-purpose flour
1 teaspoon baking powder
½ teaspoon baking soda
   Dash of salt
2 large ripe bananas
1 egg
½ cup packed brown sugar
½ cup plain yogurt
¼ cup butter, softened
1 teaspoon vanilla extract
   Frosting of your choice (optional; pages 185–188)

Preheat the oven to 350°F. Grease a 9" × 9" baking pan.

In a large bowl, whisk together the flour, baking powder, baking soda, and salt. In a large bowl, with an electric mixer on medium speed, beat the bananas until smooth (the smoother the bananas, the lighter your cake). Beat in the egg, brown sugar, yogurt, butter, and vanilla until blended. Gradually stir in the flour mixture until blended.

Pour into the prepared baking pan. Bake for 30 minutes or until a toothpick inserted in the center comes out clean. Remove from the oven and cool on a rack for 10 minutes. Remove the cake to the rack and cool completely. Frost if desired and cut into 16 squares.

Makes 16 squares

EASY FROSTING

1 cup butter
2 cups confectioners' sugar
2 tablespoons milk
1 teaspoon vanilla extract

In a medium bowl, using an electric mixer, beat the butter until blended. Beat in the confectioners' sugar, milk, and vanilla until fluffy and smooth.

Makes 1½ cups, enough to generously frost a 9" × 9" cake or 12 cupcakes

VANILLA CREAM CHEESE FROSTING

It was a challenge to create frostings without the usual 2–4 cups of sugar most recipes call for. The volume in this rich frosting is created by the vigorously whipped cream cheese. At least you can skip the hand weights at the gym today.

> 4 ounces cream cheese
> 2 tablespoons butter
> ¾ cup confectioners' sugar
> ¼ cup milk
> 1 teaspoon vanilla extract

In a medium bowl, with an electric mixer on medium-high speed, beat the cream cheese and butter until blended. Beat in the confectioners' sugar, milk, and vanilla until fluffy and smooth and doubled in volume.

Makes about 1½ cups, enough to generously frost a 9" × 9" cake or 12 cupcakes

PEANUT BUTTER FROSTING

¼ cup butter

2 heaping tablespoons creamy natural peanut butter

1 cup confectioners' sugar

¼ cup milk

In a medium bowl, with an electric mixer at medium speed, beat the butter and peanut butter until blended. Beat in the confectioners' sugar and milk until fluffy and smooth and doubled in volume.

Makes about 1 cup

JAM FROSTING

This frosting requires just ½ cup of confectioners' sugar. Its sweet, fruity flavor and pretty colors come from your favorite jam, jelly, or marmalade. Orange marmalade is particularly yummy and has a lovely summery hue.

4 ounces cream cheese
¼ cup butter
½ cup confectioners' sugar
½ cup milk
2 heaping tablespoons your favorite fruit juice–sweetened jam, jelly, or marmalade

In a medium bowl, with an electric mixer at medium speed, beat the cream cheese and butter until blended. Beat in the confectioners' sugar, milk, and jam, jelly, or marmalade until fluffy and smooth and doubled in volume.

Makes about 1½ cups

S'MORES

I've seen quite a few parents go wide eyed when a tray of s'mores appears. This classic campfire treat is about as easy and economical as dessert can get.

20 graham cracker sheets (4 crackers to a sheet)
10 large marshmallows, each cut in half
20 small pieces of chocolate (2 chocolate bars broken into small pieces will do) or ⅔ cup chocolate chips

Preheat the oven to 350°F.

Break each graham cracker sheet in half and arrange on a baking sheet lined with parchment paper. Top half of the crackers with a marshmallow half and top the remaining crackers with chocolate pieces or chips. Use the chocolate sparingly. Too much will result in a gooey mess, which is great when you're 10, but not so great when you're the parent of a 2-year-old.

Bake for 5 minutes, or until the marshmallows and chocolate are melted. Remove from the oven and quickly sandwich a marshmallow cracker with a chocolate cracker. Gently press together and serve.

Makes 20 s'mores

PARTY PLANNING

Keep it fun. Keep it simple. Give in to your inner child when planning your own child's birthday party. Fun, wacky themes for activities and treats can make each birthday memorable without expensive catering or party planners. Up until your child is 3, he probably will not care if his party theme is Barney or Beethoven. To indulge your own sense of whimsy, however, be creative—there will be cute photographs after all. Some simple themes for toddlers that are easy to execute are:

- Any sort of transportation: cars, planes, trains, boats, etc.
- Animals
- A favorite color or shape
- Letters and numbers

Don't run yourself ragged trying to create a wonderland of party favors. Rather than searching all over town for perfectly matching napkins and plates with that very specific train design, consider having one or two very cool theme items like a cake or cookies in the shape of a train and just coordinating the colors of the rest of the party goods.

There are certain "rules" to keep in mind when planning this all-important event.

- Keep it short. Two hours is usually the outer limit for kids up to 4 or 5 years old.

- Keep it small, especially for the first and second birthdays. Let's face it—there will be many opportunities to invite his or her entire class over in the years to come.

- Plan it around a mealtime. Having even a simple lunch is a built-in activity, and even if the main culinary event at your party is cake, you definitely don't want a group of sugar-happy children who've eaten only cake.

- Play it safe. When your guests RSVP, ask about food allergies.

- Let it be the special occasion that it is. This is the time for fun sandwiches, snacks, and treats. Don't get hung up on the crudité platter.

- Don't go overboard on the sugar. I've found that certain foods (like frostings) really do require some amount of sugar for taste and texture. But moderate that with a low-sugar cake recipe or just use smaller amounts to ice your cakes. Watch out for sprinkles and jimmies—pure sugar.

Ice Cream Sandwiches

These petite ice cream sandwiches are made from your homemade cookies and your favorite store-bought ice cream.

> 12 Gingersnaps (page 152) or Egg-Free Shortbread Cookies (page 150)
> Vanilla or your favorite flavor ice cream, slightly softened

Use a melon baller to scoop even portions of ice cream. Place 1–2 scoops of ice cream on the flat side of a cookie and top with another cookie. Press gently. Repeat with the remaining cookies and ice cream. Arrange the sandwiches in a pie or cake pan. Cover with aluminum foil and freeze at least 30 minutes or until set.

Makes 6 sandwiches

Yogurt Parfait

For very special occasions, treat your guests to these parfaits served in plastic wine or champagne glasses. Otherwise, clear plastic cups will do fine to show off the layers of colors and flavors.

1   cup plain or vanilla yogurt
3   tablespoons fruit juice–sweetened strawberry jam
2   tablespoons chocolate syrup or fruit juice–sweetened blueberry jam
Whipped cream (optional)
Chopped nuts (optional)

In a clear cup or glass, spoon in alternating layers ⅓ cup yogurt, 2 tablespoons strawberry jam, ⅓ cup yogurt, chocolate syrup or blueberry jam, then the remaining ⅓ cup yogurt. Top with the remaining 1 tablespoon strawberry jam and if you'd like, a dollop of whipped cream and a sprinkle of nuts.

Serve with a spoon.

Makes 1 parfait

Milk Shakes

Here's a great example of how to make a decadent treat kid-friendly. Use a little less ice cream, add in some yogurt, and definitely skip the sugary syrups. If you have an undeniable request for chocolate milk shakes, add just 1 tablespoon syrup for each shake.

> 1 scoop vanilla ice cream or frozen yogurt
> ½ cup plain yogurt
> ½ cup milk

1 of these flavorings:

> Handful hulled strawberries, blueberries, or any berry
> ½ sliced peach
> ½ banana
> 2 tablespoons fruit juice–sweetened jam or jelly
> 1 tablespoon maple syrup or honey
> 1 tablespoon chocolate syrup

In a blender, puree the ice cream or frozen yogurt, yogurt, milk, and 1 of the flavorings until smooth.

Makes 1 milk shake

FRESH JUICE POPS

I hope parents still make juice pops for their children on hot summer days. They are so easy to make and also make a great kid activity in the kitchen. Juice pops can be made in any small, freezer-safe container: ice cube trays, small paper cups, even clean juice boxes.

> 2 cups your favorite juice (orange, pineapple, and cranberry result in very vibrant colors)
> 2 cups water
> Wooden pop sticks

In a 1½-quart pitcher, stir together the juice and water. Pour into molds and cover each with plastic wrap. Insert sticks through the plastic wrap (that's what will keep them upright) in the center of each mold. Freeze until set, about 2 hours for ice cube trays and longer for cups.

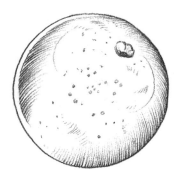

BANANA SPLITS

What's a surefire recipe for a splitting headache? How about a party full of hyper, sugar-happy toddlers? The only sugar in this recipe is that found in the frozen yogurt or sorbet you buy at the store. The "syrups" mimic in appearance traditionally syrupy ice cream toppings.

1 small ripe banana
Frozen yogurt or sorbet
Faux caramel syrup (recipe below)
Strawberry syrup (recipe below)
Blueberry syrup (recipe on the opposite page)
2 teaspoons finely chopped walnuts (omit if your baby or guests are allergic)

To make the syrups:

For faux caramel: Put 2 pitted apricots in a steamer basket in a medium pot with 1" water. Cover and bring to a boil over medium-high heat. Reduce the heat to medium and steam for 10 minutes or until soft but not mushy. Uncover and let cool slightly in the pot. In a blender, puree to a thin, pourable consistency.

For strawberry: In a blender, puree ¼ cup hulled strawberries to a thin, pourable consistency.

For blueberry: In a blender, puree ¼ cup blueberries to a thin, pourable consistency.

To assemble the banana splits:

Slice the banana lengthwise and then in half crosswise. Place 2 quarters in each of 2 shallow bowls.

Using a melon baller, spoon 4 or 5 scoops frozen yogurt over the banana in each bowl.

Drizzle 1 tablespoon of each syrup over the yogurt scoops, keeping the colors distinct from each other.

Top each with 1 teaspoon of the chopped walnuts.

Makes 2 splits

BISTRO BITS

- Assembling the banana splits can be fun for the parents, and your tots will be fascinated as they watch the shapes and colors come together.
- This recipe is a snap to double or triple depending on the size of your party.
- Sorbet is a great idea if some of your guests are dairy sensitive. But be sure to read the ingredients for traces of milk proteins.
- Some children are so allergic to nuts that they cannot even touch them. It's worth a few phone calls to make absolutely sure your guests are okay with your menu.

SLUSHIES

A cool, soothing treat for swollen, teething gums and also a great hot-weather cooler. Serve these in small quantities—eating too much ice can cause stomachaches.

> Orange juice
> Cranberry juice
> Ice cubes

Fill 1 ice cube tray with orange juice and another with cranberry juice; freeze until set, about 2 hours. In a blender, crush equal amounts orange juice cubes and ice cubes; spoon into clear plastic cups. Then crush equal amounts cranberry juice cubes and ice cubes; spoon on top of the orange slush for a very tropical-looking treat.

BISTRO BITS: Serve these with straws or little umbrellas if you are feeling especially festive.

VANILLA PUDDING

4 egg yolks
½ cup sugar
2 cups milk
¼ cup all-purpose flour
1 tablespoon butter
1 tablespoon vanilla extract

In a medium bowl, whisk together the egg yolks and sugar until it falls in ribbons from the whisk. Whisk in the milk and flour until blended. Set a heatproof bowl over a saucepan that's been filled with about 2" water. Bring the water to a boil over medium-high heat. Pour the egg mixture into the bowl and cook, whisking constantly, for 5 minutes or just until the pudding boils around the edges. As the pudding heats up it will be lumpy at first, then it will smooth out. Be careful not to burn the bottom of the pudding. Carefully re-move the bowl from the saucepan and whisk in the butter and vanilla. Cool slightly, then spoon into small bowls or an airtight container. Place plastic wrap directly on the surface of the pudding to prevent that unappealing "skin" from forming. Chill until ready to serve.

Makes about 2 cups

RICE PUDDING

There must have been a lot of terrible rice pudding going around in the '70s. So many of my friends grimace at the mention of it. Be that as it may, this recipe produces a lightly sweet rice pudding that's not at all heavy, and you can add in the raisins if you wish at the end.

2 cups milk
½ cup cooked rice
2 tablespoons packed brown sugar
1 teaspoon ground cinnamon
½ cup chopped raisins (optional)

In a medium saucepan, heat the milk and rice over low heat, stirring occasionally, for up to 30 minutes or until the rice has absorbed most of the milk. Remove from the heat and stir in the sugar, cinnamon, and raisins, if using. Cool and serve.

Makes about 2 cups

SAMPLE MENU

Here's a sample menu for your little guests.

**Snacks to put out while guests
arrive and play**

Cut-up vegetables and fruit

Cheese cubes

Animal crackers

Sourdough Crisps (page 156)

Cinnamon Crisps (page 155)

Simple lunch ideas

Tea Sandwiches (page 86)

Cheese Quesadillas (page 84)

Mini Burgers (page 89)

Macaroni and Cheese (page 120)

Dessert and treats

Banana Cake (page 184)

Yogurt Parfait (page 193)

Ice Cream Sandwiches (page 192)

S'mores (page 189)

Beverages

Watermelon Aqua Fresca (page 171)

Baby Bellinis (page 166)

Orangeade (page 162)

Strawberry Punch (page 173)

INDEX

Underscored page references indicate boxed text or Bistro Bits tips.

Conversion Chart

These equivalents have been slightly rounded to make measuring easier.

VOLUME MEASUREMENTS

U.S.	Imperial	Metric
¼ tsp	–	1 ml
½ tsp	–	2 ml
1 tsp	–	5 ml
1 Tbsp	–	15 ml
2 Tbsp (1 oz)	1 fl oz	30 ml
¼ cup (2 oz)	2 fl oz	60 ml
⅓ cup (3 oz)	3 fl oz	80 ml
½ cup (4 oz)	4 fl oz	120 ml
⅔ cup (5 oz)	5 fl oz	160 ml
¾ cup (6 oz)	6 fl oz	180 ml
1 cup (8 oz)	8 fl oz	240 ml

WEIGHT MEASUREMENTS

U.S.	Metric
1 oz	30 g
2 oz	60 g
4 oz (¼ lb)	115 g
5 oz (⅓ lb)	145 g
6 oz	170 g
7 oz	200 g
8 oz (½ lb)	230 g
10 oz	285 g
12 oz (¾ lb)	340 g
14 oz	400 g
16 oz (1 lb)	455 g
2.2 lb	1 kg

LENGTH MEASUREMENTS

U.S.	Metric
¼"	0.6 cm
½"	1.25 cm
1"	2.5 cm
2"	5 cm
4"	11 cm
6"	15 cm
8"	20 cm
10"	25 cm
12" (1')	30 cm

PAN SIZES

U.S.	Metric
8" cake pan	20 × 4 cm sandwich or cake tin
9" cake pan	23 × 3.5 cm sandwich or cake tin
11" × 7" baking pan	28 × 18 cm baking tin
13" × 9" baking pan	32.5 × 23 cm baking tin
15" × 10" baking pan	38 × 25.5 cm baking tin (Swiss roll tin)
1½ qt baking dish	1.5 liter baking dish
2 qt baking dish	2 liter baking dish
2 qt rectangular baking dish	30 × 19 cm baking dish
9" pie plate	22 × 4 or 23 × 4 cm pie plate
7" or 8" springform pan	18 or 20 cm springform or loose-bottom cake tin
9" × 5" loaf pan	23 × 13 cm or 2 lb narrow loaf tin or pâté tin

TEMPERATURES

Fahrenheit	Centigrade	Gas
140°	60°	–
160°	70°	–
180°	80°	–
225°	105°	¼
250°	120°	½
275°	135°	1
300°	150°	2
325°	160°	3
350°	180°	4
375°	190°	5
400°	200°	6
425°	220°	7
450°	230°	8
475°	245°	9
500°	260°	–